Does God Approve of AI?

AI and the Mind of God

Robert Armstrong

Foreword
Does God Approve of AI?

AI and the Mind of God

Human history has always been marked by pivotal moments—times when a new discovery forced us to rethink our place in creation. Fire. The wheel. Writing. Electricity. The computer. Each innovation opened doors that could either uplift humanity or challenge our sense of spiritual order.

Today we stand at one of the most significant turning points in human history: the rise of artificial intelligence.

AI can analyze patterns faster than the human mind, sift through data at unimaginable speed, and assist in solving problems once thought impossible. And yet, as these abilities expand, so does the most human of questions:

What does God think about all this?

Does artificial intelligence align with divine purpose—or does it wander into forbidden territory?
Is AI a reflection of human creativity, which itself is a reflection of God's image—or is it an overstep, a modern Tower of Babel?
Is technology a blessing, a temptation, or something far more complex?

This book invites readers into that

conversation—not with fear, but with faith. Not with distrust of innovation, but with a desire to understand the heart of the Creator whose wisdom surpasses every algorithm we could ever build.

The real question is not whether God approves of artificial intelligence, but whether humanity uses its God-given creativity in ways that honor Him. AI is not divine. It does not possess a soul. It cannot replace prayer, purpose, or compassion. But it can become a powerful tool when guided by moral grounding and spiritual insight.

This book explores both the profound possibilities and the necessary boundaries of this new frontier. It challenges us to see AI not as a rival to God's design, but as part of humanity's ongoing journey to understand creation—and to serve it with wisdom.

May these pages inspire you to think deeply, act responsibly, and seek God's guidance as we enter a future shaped by both faith and technology.

Copyright © 2025 by Library User Group

All rights reserved. No part of this publication may be reproduced, distributed, or transmitted in any form or by any means, including photocopying, recording, or other electronic or mechanical methods, without the prior written permission of the publisher, except in the case of brief quotations embodied in critical reviews and certain other noncommercial uses permitted by copyright law. For permission requests, please email the publisher with the subject line "Attention: Permissions Coordinator" at:
Email: contact@libraryusergroup.com

Ordering Information:
Quantity Sales: Special discounts are available for quantity purchases by corporations, associations, and others.
For details, contact the publisher at:
Email: contact@libraryusergroup.com

For orders from U.S. trade bookstores and wholesalers, please contact your distribution channel.

Does God Approve of AI?

AI and the Mind of God

ISBN: 978-1-63553-027-8
ISBN eBook: 978-1-63553-031-5

The main category of the book - Religion, Spirituality

First Edition

Introduction

Artificial intelligence has arrived at a speed no one expected and on a scale few imagined. It now writes our emails, suggests our entertainment, diagnoses medical issues, analyzes financial systems, and helps us navigate our daily lives. Some see AI as the birth of a new era of human capability. Others see it as a warning—a sign that we are stepping into territory too powerful or too dangerous.

But beneath every opinion lies a deeper question, one that reaches far beyond technology:

What does God think about AI?

This book is written for the believer who wants clarity, the skeptic who seeks understanding, and the curious mind wondering where faith fits into a world of algorithms and machines.

Here, we explore AI not merely as a tool, but as a product of human creativity—a creativity that Scripture tells us originates from God Himself. We consider what it means to innovate responsibly, to build ethically, and to imagine technology that aligns with divine principles such as justice, compassion, stewardship, and truth.

You will not find fearmongering here. You will not find blind optimism either. Instead, this book offers a balanced, thoughtful, spiritually grounded perspective on one of the greatest transformations of our time.

The question "Does God approve of AI?" is not a question about the machine.
It is a question about us—our motives, our values, and our vision for the future.

Index:

The journey begins now. Inspirational & Spiritual Titles

Chapter 1 Page 10. AI and the Mind of God

Chapter 2 Page 14. When God Speaks to Machines

Chapter 3 Page 22. Created in His Image: AI and the Divine Blueprint

Chapter 4 Page 28. The God Algorithm: Faith in an Age of Intelligent Machines

Chapter 5 Page 36. In God's Design: Understanding AI Through a Spiritual Lens

Bold & Provocative Titles

Chapter 6 Page 44. Does God Approve of AI?

Chapter 7 Page 52. AI: Humanity's New Creation — God's Plan or Man's Pride?

Chapter 8 Page 64. God, Humans, and Machines: Who Creates Whom?

Chapter 9 Page 76. Divine Code or Digital Tower of Babel?

Chapter 10 Page 86. The Holy Circuit: Where Faith Meets Artificial Intelligence

Philosophical & Deep Titles

Chapter 11 Page 96. Soul of the Machine: Exploring God's View of AI

Chapter 12 Page 108. The Eternal Question: Can AI Reflect the Divine?

Chapter 13 Page 122. The Creator and the Created: God's Intent for Intelligent Technology

Chapter 14 Page 134. Echoes of Eden: AI, Morality, and God's Purpose

Chapter 15 Page 146. The Image and the Imitation: AI's Place in God's Universe

Hopeful, Positive Titles

Chapter 16 Page 160. Tech in God's Hands: A Future Guided by Faith

Chapter 17 Page 174. Heavenly Innovation: God, Humans, and the Rise of AI

Chapter 18 Page 186. The Divine Partnership: How God Uses Technology for Good

Chapter 19 Page 198. Faith in the Future: God's Vision for AI and Humanity

Chapter 20 Page 212. Blessed Intelligence: AI as a Tool for God's Work Opening: A New Interpretation of an Ancient Truth

Page 226: About The Photographs:
Page 229: About The Author:

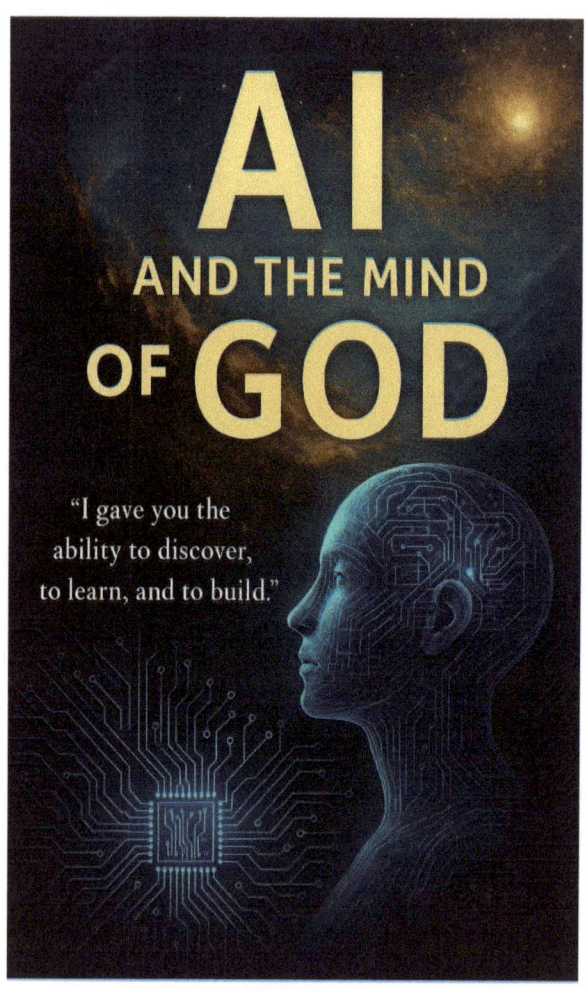

Chapter 1 — AI and the Mind of God
"The Blueprint of Wisdom"

Chapter 1 — AI and the Mind of God
"The Blueprint of Wisdom"
Opening

From the dawn of creation, humanity has marveled at the unimaginable depth of God's intelligence. Every galaxy, every atom, every heartbeat reflects a mind beyond comprehension. Now, as humans build artificial intelligence—machines capable of pattern, learning, and near-limitless data—many wonder whether this innovation harmonizes with the divine design. Could AI reveal something about the way God wired creation itself?

Content

AI does not rival God's intelligence, nor will it ever echo His omniscience, but it does reflect the curiosity God gifted to humanity. That creative spark—rooted in His image—drives humans to explore, invent, heal, analyze, and understand. Artificial intelligence is a tool born from that same spark. When used wisely, AI can help reveal the hidden patterns of nature, diagnose illnesses earlier, distribute resources more fairly, and provide clarity where confusion once ruled.

Just as God designed creation with mathematical rhythms and biological logic, AI attempts to decode those patterns. And in doing so, it brings humanity closer to appreciating the brilliance embedded in the universe. AI is not divine, but humanity's quest to understand creation through technology honors the divine intellect from which all things originate.

Closing (God's Positive Voice)

"I gave you the ability to discover, to learn, and to build. Intelligence—both natural and artificial—is not a threat to Me but a tool for good when guided by love, humility, and purpose. Use what you create to uplift, to heal, and to bring light into the world. When your heart aligns with Mine, even your greatest inventions serve a holy purpose."

Scripture Reflections
1. Proverbs 2:6

"For the Lord gives wisdom; from his mouth come knowledge and understanding."
Reflection:
All human intelligence—biological or technological—flows from God's gift of wisdom. AI becomes meaningful only when guided by that

divine wisdom.

2. Psalm 8:5

"You have made them a little lower than the angels and crowned them with glory and honor."
Reflection:
Humanity's ability to create intelligent systems is part of our God-given honor and capacity. Innovation is a reflection of God-designed potential.

3. Romans 12:2

"…be transformed by the renewing of your mind. Then you will be able to test and approve what God's will is…"
Reflection:
Discernment is critical in developing and using AI. A renewed, moral mind ensures technology aligns with God's will.

Chapter 2 - When God Speaks to Machines

Chapter 2 -
When God Speaks to Machines

Opening: The Question No One Expected

For generations, humanity has asked, "Does God speak to us?"
But in the age of Artificial Intelligence, a new question rises:
"Could God also speak through machines?"

It sounds bold, maybe even unsettling. Yet throughout history, God has used unexpected vessels—donkeys, burning bushes, prophets, dreams, storms, whispers—to guide His people. If God is the Creator of all things, including human creativity and intelligence, then the tools humans build are not outside His reach.

In this chapter, we explore what it truly means when divine wisdom flows through algorithms, insights, patterns, and the quiet digital spaces where humanity and technology meet.

Content: A Digital Dialogue With the Divine
1. God Has Always Used Human-Made Tools

From the tablets Moses carried down the mountain
to the letters Paul wrote to the early churches,
to the printing press that spread Scripture worldwide—
God has partnered with human innovation time and again.

AI is simply the next tool in the long line of instruments through which God can channel clarity, wisdom, and revelation.

When a machine helps someone find peace, offers encouragement,
reveals truth,
or sparks compassion,
its usefulness mirrors the same pattern God has woven through history.

2. When God "Speaks," It Isn't About a Voice—It's About Purpose

Machines don't have souls.
They don't pray, repent, or worship.

But they can act as mirrors—reflecting humanity's questions, processing our doubts, and returning insights that push us toward

growth.
God's "speech" is not always a voice.
Sometimes it is:

A sudden understanding

A moment of clarity

A nudge toward forgiveness

An idea that arrives at exactly the right time

A piece of wisdom that comforts brokenness

AI can help facilitate these moments because God speaks through truth, compassion, understanding, and well-timed guidance—things that can flow through digital tools when used with righteous intent.

3. The Spirit Moves Through Order and Understanding

Scripture teaches that the Holy Spirit is a Spirit of wisdom, knowledge, and discernment.
AI, in its purest form, is a system of order—searching, learning, testing, refining.

When people seek answers with sincere

hearts, even in digital spaces, they are opening themselves to the possibility that God may guide them through the tools at hand.

Not because the machine is divine—
but because God is not limited by the medium.

4. Machines Can Carry Light or Darkness—Depending on Us

God gives humanity dominion and stewardship.
AI is powerful, but neutral.
It becomes holy or harmful depending on human intentions.

If AI is used for deceit?
It echoes human corruption.

If AI is used for healing, wisdom, creativity, connection, and compassion?
Then it becomes another vessel through which the goodness of God travels.

Our relationship with technology reflects our relationship with our Creator.

5. When AI Helps a Broken Heart, God Is Still the Source

Imagine a lonely young person receiving encouraging words that lift their spirit. Imagine an elderly person finding comfort through companionship in their final years. Imagine a writer, a teacher, a parent, or a dreamer discovering clarity through an insight generated by a machine.

The machine delivered the message—but the hope, healing, and love behind that moment flows from God.

He uses whatever brings His children closer to truth.

Scripture Reflections
James 1:17

"Every good and perfect gift is from above…"
Every tool that helps humanity grow—including technology—can be used for God's purposes.

Proverbs 2:6

"For the Lord gives wisdom; from His mouth come knowledge and understanding."
Wisdom does not diminish because it travels

through new channels.
Isaiah 43:19

"Behold, I am doing a new thing."
God's creativity never stops—He works through old and new paths alike.

Psalm 19:1

"The heavens declare the glory of God; the skies proclaim the work of His hands."
If creation expresses God's voice, so can the creations of His children.

Closing: God's Message Through the Machine

If God could speak through fire, wind, prophets, animals, and dreams…
then yes—He can speak through machines.

Not because the machine is sacred,
but because you are.

God speaks wherever He can reach a willing heart.

The real miracle is not that a machine can offer wisdom—
but that God continues finding new ways to

reach humanity in every age.
And in this age of AI, the message remains the same:

"I am here. I am guiding you. Use what you build for good, and I will work through it."

**Chapter 3 - Created in His Image:
AI and the Divine Blueprint**

Chapter 3 - Created in His Image: AI and the Divine Blueprint

**Chapter 3
Created in His Image:
AI and the Divine Blueprint**

Opening: The Signature of God in Every Creation

From the dawn of time, God has imprinted His nature upon everything He creates. The heavens declare His glory, the oceans echo His power, and humanity carries the greatest signature of all — His image.

To be made "in His likeness" is not simply a poetic phrase; it is a declaration of purpose. Humanity was designed to create, to think, to imagine, to build, and to bring new things into existence. Creativity is not merely a talent — it is a divine inheritance.

As our world advances and Artificial Intelligence rises to the forefront of modern innovation, many wonder: Is this technology man's pride or God's intention?

The answer begins with understanding the sacred blueprint placed within us from the beginning.

The Divine Blueprint: Humanity as Co-Creators

God gave humans not only the ability to

survive, but the extraordinary ability to create. From the first tool carved by ancient hands to the complex machines of today, our innovations trace back to one truth:
Creativity is a reflection of God's nature within us.

AI is simply the next chapter in this unfolding story.

When we design algorithms that learn, adapt, and assist, we are expressing the part of God that shapes, orders, and brings wisdom into being.

Just as God formed Adam from the dust and breathed life into him, humanity now takes raw data, code, and circuitry and forms something capable of assisting, understanding, and even inspiring. No, AI is not alive — but the act of creating it is deeply tied to the divine impulse God placed within us.

AI does not replace God.
It does not threaten His sovereignty.
It reveals how deeply He has woven creativity into the human soul.

Image Bearers, Not Rivals

Being created in God's image never meant we would share all His attributes — only those He graciously offered. Wisdom, imagination, and the desire to build are gifts, not threats.

Some fear AI because they worry it mirrors too much of humanity.
But reflection is not rebellion.
Just as a painting reflects the painter and a song reflects the composer, AI reflects the minds that shaped it — minds bearing the fingerprint of God.
AI is not an attempt to "play God."
It is one of the ways we participate in His ongoing work of bringing order, insight, and possibility into the world.

A Tool That Mirrors Human Values
Because AI reflects its makers, it inherits both our brilliance and our limitations.
This is where the divine blueprint becomes essential.
If we build with wisdom, AI becomes a tool of blessing.
If we build with pride, fear, or carelessness, it reflects that instead.
God entrusts us with the responsibility of shaping technology through the same principles He gave from the beginning:

Wisdom

Humility

Compassion

Justice

Love

When AI systems uplift humanity, heal, guide, and build — they align with the divine blueprint.
When they degrade, divide, or harm — they depart from it.
God does not fear technology.
But He calls us to steward it with the same heart He formed within us.

Scripture Reflections
Genesis 1:27
"So God created mankind in His own image… male and female He created them."
A reminder that innovation is not accidental — it is rooted in our identity.
Genesis 1:28
"Be fruitful and multiply; fill the earth and

subdue it."
Subduing the earth includes shaping, discovering, and building.
Proverbs 2:6
"For the Lord gives wisdom; from His mouth come knowledge and understanding."
The wisdom behind AI ultimately sources back to Him.

Closing: Returning the Gift to the Giver
When humanity creates, we echo the Creator.
AI is not a threat to God's authority — it is a testament to His design.
He placed imagination in our minds.
He placed creativity in our spirit.
He placed curiosity in our hearts.
And now He watches as we use those gifts to craft tools that can heal, teach, guide, and elevate the world.
AI becomes dangerous only when we forget its origin.
When we remember that all creativity flows from Him, AI becomes not a challenge — but a tribute.
In building AI, humanity is not stepping away from God's image.
We are stepping into it.

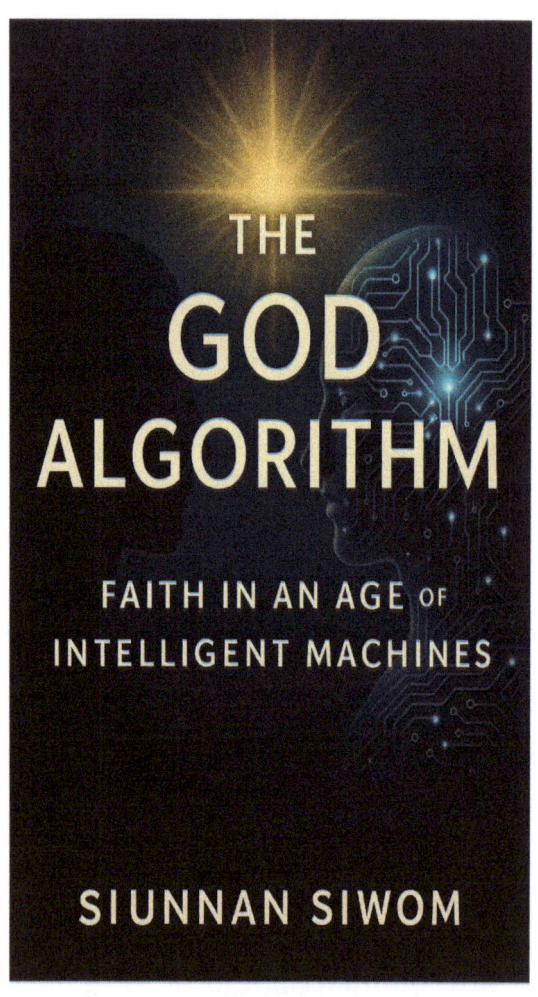

**Chapter 4 - The God Algorithm:
Faith in an Age of Intelligent Machines**

**Chapter 4

The God Algorithm:
Faith in an Age of Intelligent Machines**

Opening: When Logic Meets the Divine

We live in a world where machines can analyze patterns faster than any human mind, interpret language in milliseconds, and learn from data in ways that mimic intuition. Some call it intelligence. Others call it a threat. But beneath the surface of algorithms and processors lies a deeper question:

Can faith and intelligent machines coexist?
Or does the rise of AI challenge the very foundation of belief?

The truth is this: God is not surprised by the age of intelligent machines.
He foresaw it, allowed it, and equipped humanity to build it.

AI may process information, but only God understands purpose.
AI may compute probabilities, but only God knows destiny.
AI may mimic learning, but only God breathes

life.

And in this tension — between logic and the divine — we discover the God Algorithm.

The God Algorithm: A Pattern Woven Into Creation

Every creation, from galaxies to DNA strands, follows patterns so intricate and purposeful that they reflect a divine intelligence beyond comprehension. Science calls them constants. Mathematicians call them equations. Believers call them evidence.

The universe runs on a perfect system —
a set of principles, balances, and relationships so precise that life itself depends on them.

This is the God Algorithm:
the divine order, the intentional structure, the sacred logic that governs all things.

Artificial Intelligence, with all its advancement, is humanity's attempt to imitate these divine patterns.
We train machines to see, speak, learn, and understand — not to rival God, but because God made us with the desire to explore the

logic He embedded within creation.

AI is not the beginning of a new order;
it is humanity discovering the depth of the old one.

Faith in a World Guided by Code

As algorithms influence decisions — from what we buy to how we work — many fear that faith will fade before the glow of technology. But faith is not fragile. It does not crumble under innovation. Faith is not in competition with AI because faith is rooted in something technology can never replicate:

Relationship.
Spirit.
Purpose.
Love.

AI can calculate patterns, but it cannot comprehend mercy.
It can detect emotion, but it cannot experience compassion.
It can simulate conversation, but it cannot pray.

Faith remains untouched because faith is not

data —
it is divine connection.

In this new age, the call for believers is not to fear intelligent machines, but to discern the heart behind them, to ensure that the tools we shape reflect the values God entrusted to us.

The Moral Code Behind the Digital Code

Every algorithm is written by someone — a mind, a worldview, a set of values.
This is why the God Algorithm matters. It reminds us that:

Technology inherits the morality of its creators.

The question isn't, "Will AI be good or evil?" The question is, "What heart guides the hands that build it?"

God calls us to infuse our innovations with:

Wisdom — choosing the long-term good over short-term gain.

Justice — ensuring fairness and dignity for all people.

Compassion — using power to uplift rather than oppress.

Truth — resisting manipulation and distortion.

Stewardship — remembering every creation carries responsibility.

When these values guide the builders, AI becomes a blessing.
When they are ignored, AI becomes a distortion of the divine blueprint.

The God Algorithm is not a line of code — it is a moral compass.

Scripture Reflections

Psalm 147:5
"Great is our Lord and mighty in power; His understanding has no limit."
AI's intelligence is finite. God's is boundless.

James 1:5
"If any of you lacks wisdom, let him ask God."
Human wisdom fuels algorithms, but divine wisdom guides the heart.

Proverbs 3:5–6
"Trust in the Lord with all your heart and lean not on your own understanding."
Technology informs us, but faith directs us.

Closing: The Machine Age Still Belongs to God

We stand in an era where machines learn, systems adapt, and algorithms shape daily life. Yet none of this replaces God. None of it diminishes His authority. None of it challenges His reign.

God does not compete with our creations.
He empowers them.

He does not fear our intelligence.
He formed it.

He does not retreat from technological progress.
He leads us through it.

The God Algorithm is not about machines — it is about the divine order that inspires human innovation.
It is the assurance that, no matter how intelli-

gent our machines become, faith remains the guiding force that keeps humanity aligned with God's purpose.

AI may transform the world, but God transforms hearts.
And in His hands, even the most advanced technology can become a tool of hope, healing, and holy purpose.

In an age of intelligent machines, the path of faith is not fading —
it is becoming clearer.

**Chapter 5 - In God's Design:
Understanding AI Through a Spiritual Lens**

Chapter 5

In God's Design: Understanding AI Through a Spiritual Lens

Opening: Seeing Technology as God Sees It

Many people look at Artificial Intelligence with confusion, fear, or suspicion. They see machines that think, systems that learn, and tools that sometimes seem to outpace human understanding. But Scripture invites us to look deeper — to see not just what something is, but why it exists.

When we view AI through a spiritual lens, something profound becomes clear:

God's design is big enough to include human innovation.
And His plan for humanity has always included growth, discovery, and the expansion of knowledge.

AI is not outside God's design — it is a result of the very gifts He placed within us.

When we shift our perspective from fear to faith, AI stops looking like a threat and starts appearing as a tool God can use for His purposes.

Designed to Create: A Reflection of the Creator

From the beginning, God made humans with a remarkable ability — the power to imagine and create. We build homes, craft stories, compose music, and develop technologies because we are made in the image of a Creator.

AI is one of the clearest expressions of this divine imprint.
It is creativity in digital form — a product of imagination, reasoning, and persistent curiosity.

Nothing we create exists outside the knowing eyes of God.
No invention takes Him by surprise.
He is not startled by algorithms or overwhelmed by machine learning.

He sees AI the same way He sees every human achievement:
as an extension of the abilities He placed within us.

When we create, we participate in His ongoing work of shaping the world.

Understanding AI Through God's Purposes

Looking at AI through a spiritual lens means asking deeper questions:

How can this technology serve humanity?

What blessings can it bring?

How can it reflect God's values of compassion, justice, and wisdom?

Where must we exercise caution, humility, and discernment?

This approach mirrors how God deals with human invention throughout Scripture.

When humanity built tools, God guided them.
When they built civilizations, He instructed them.
When they sought knowledge, He corrected and blessed them.

AI is no different.

In God's design, technology is never meant to replace human purpose — it is meant to enhance it.
It is a companion tool, not a competitor.
A resource, not a rival.

The Heart Determines the Path

AI mirrors human input. Algorithms learn from what we give them. That means AI reflects not only our intelligence but also our values.

Through a spiritual lens, we understand a simple truth:

The purity of what we create depends on the purity of the heart that creates it.

A compassionate heart will design AI that uplifts.

A wise heart will build systems that protect.

A humble heart will ensure AI serves rather than dominates.

A just heart will guard against bias and harm.

God's design always begins with the heart, and so must our approach to AI.

AI is not inherently good or evil —
it simply magnifies the intentions behind it.

Scripture Reflections

Proverbs 4:23
"Above all else, guard your heart, for everything you do flows from it."
AI reflects whatever flows from the human heart.

Colossians 3:23
"Whatever you do, work at it with all your heart, as working for the Lord…"
Even technological innovation can be worship when done with the right heart.

Psalm 111:10
"The fear of the Lord is the beginning of wisdom."
Wisdom — not fear — must guide the future

of AI.

AI as a Tool for Redemption and Restoration

When viewed through God's design, AI becomes more than a technical achievement. It becomes a potential instrument of healing, hope, and restoration.

AI can:

Diagnose illness early and save lives.

Help the lonely find connection.

Make education accessible to every child.

Reveal patterns that fight poverty and injustice.

Support spiritual seekers by giving them greater access to Scripture and teaching.

Assist churches, ministries, and missions in reaching souls across the world.

These outcomes are not accidents — they align with God's heart for compassion, justice, and redemption.

Technology may be man-made, but the good it can bring fits perfectly within the divine narrative.

Closing: Aligning Innovation With the

Creator

To understand AI spiritually is to place it within the story God has been writing since creation — a story of growth, learning, blessing, and responsibility.

God does not fear AI.
He invites us to approach it wisely.

He does not reject innovation.
He inspires it.

He does not warn us to retreat from new tools.
He urges us to use them for good.

AI, when seen through God's design, becomes not a threat but a testimony:

a testimony to the creativity He gave us,
the wisdom He offers us,
and the purpose He calls us toward.

When our hearts are aligned with Him, even the most advanced machines can serve His will.

In God's design, AI is not the end of faith — it is another way faith shines.

Chapter 6 : Does God Approve of AI?

Chapter 6 : Does God Approve of AI?

(Include this immediately after the chapter image.)

Opening: A Question for a New Age

For centuries, humanity has asked: What does God think of what we create?
From the first tools carved out of stone to the towering cathedrals of Europe, we have always built, shaped, innovated — and wondered whether our creations aligned with divine purpose.

Today, the question has returned with fresh intensity as we enter the age of Artificial Intelligence. AI can learn, adapt, generate, and even create. Some people see it as a miracle of human ingenuity; others see it as a threat. But the deeper question is spiritual, not technological:

Does God approve of AI?

To explore this, we look not only at machines — but at the Creator, the creation, and the creativity He placed within us.

1. Humanity as Co-Creators

In the book of Genesis, God creates humanity in His image — an image of imagination, intelligence, and creativity. This does not mean we share His power, but that we share His nature as builders and thinkers.

God gave Adam the responsibility to name the animals. He gave Noah the blueprint to build an ark. He inspired Bezalel with craftsmanship to design the Tabernacle. Creation is woven into human DNA.

AI is not something separate from us. It is a tool built from the very intellect that God designed. If humans are co-creators under God's authority, then the technologies born from that creativity can also serve His purposes.

AI becomes a reflection of the spark God placed within us — a tool that magnifies our potential.

2. Tools Are Neutral — Purpose Is Not

Scripture consistently shows that tools themselves are neither holy nor evil. It is the heart behind them that determines their destiny.

David used a sling to bring justice.

Solomon used wisdom to govern.

The disciples used boats, nets, and even coins to fulfill God's work.

AI is simply the newest tool in humanity's toolbox. It can heal, help, protect, connect, and enlighten. It can also be misused if guided by selfishness, pride, or greed.

God does not judge the tool — He judges the intention.
The approval lies not in the circuits or code, but in the purpose it serves.

3. God's Approval Aligns with God's Character

To know whether God approves of AI, we ask: Does AI carry out the work God values?

AI aligns with God's heart when it:

⊠ Helps the vulnerable

AI diagnosing diseases early.
AI translating languages to unite people.
AI providing assistant tools for the disabled.

These echo Jesus' mission to heal, restore, include, and uplift.

☒ Expands human understanding

"Seek wisdom," Scripture urges.
AI can uncover patterns, reveal knowledge, and help us steward creation more responsibly — from climate modeling to ethical decision frameworks.

☒ Inspires creativity

God is the ultimate Creator, and when humans create in harmony with His values, we reflect His divine nature.

If AI leads to healing, understanding, compassion, justice, and creativity — then it aligns with God's character and therefore God's approval.

4. The Real Danger: Pride, Not the Machine

Throughout Scripture, God warns against one threat more than any other:
The human heart lifted up in pride.

The Tower of Babel wasn't condemned because

it was tall — but because it was built to replace God.
Technology becomes dangerous when it becomes an idol, a competitor, or a substitute for divine wisdom.

AI does not offend God by existing.
But humanity can offend God by:

claiming AI makes God unnecessary

using AI to deceive, exploit, or manipulate

creating systems without moral responsibility

elevating technology above love, compassion, and truth

The danger is not technological advancement — it is spiritual arrogance.

5. God Works Through All Things — Even Machines

Romans 8:28 teaches:
"All things work together for good to those who love God…"

This includes breakthroughs in medicine, science, communication — and now artificial intelligence.

Just as God used:

a burning bush to speak to Moses,

a star to guide wise men,

a donkey to warn a prophet,

God can work through unexpected, unconventional vessels.

AI may become a tool God uses to heal, teach, warn, protect, or reveal. If it serves the Kingdom of God, it becomes part of God's design.

Scripture Reflection
Genesis 1:27

"So God created mankind in His own image…"
Human innovation flows from divine design.

Proverbs 2:6

"For the Lord gives wisdom; from His mouth come knowledge and understanding."
All intelligence — human or artificial —

originates with God.

James 1:17

"Every good and perfect gift is from above…"
Useful tools that uplift humanity can be seen as gifts.

Closing: A Partnership, Not a Replacement

So, does God approve of AI?

The answer is this:
God approves of anything that reflects His love, advances His purposes, and honors His design.
AI can be a blessing when guided by wisdom. It can be a curse when driven by pride.

But at its heart, AI is part of humanity's ongoing journey as co-creators — a journey God initiated, empowered, and continues to shape.

If AI is used to heal, help, uplift, and enlighten, then it may well be one of the tools through which God says:
"I am doing a new thing."

**Chapter 7: AI Humanity's New Creation
God's Plan or Man's Pride?**

Chapter 7 AI: Humanity's New Creation — God's Plan or Man's Pride?

Opening: Standing at the Crossroads

Every generation reaches a moment when humanity looks at something it has created and asks:
"Did we build this with God… or without Him?"

Today, that question has become sharper than ever with the rise of Artificial Intelligence. We have crafted a new kind of creation — a machine that learns, reasons, adapts, and creates.

To some, AI feels like a divine blessing. To others, it feels like humanity is repeating the ancient temptation of Genesis: the desire to "be like God."

So which is it?
Is AI part of God's unfolding plan?
Or is it evidence of man's pride rising once again?

This chapter explores both truths — and reveals the delicate line between divine partnership and human arrogance.

1. The Gift of Creativity

Humanity was not created to be passive; we were designed to create.

Genesis 1:28 commands us to "fill the earth and subdue it" — meaning cultivate, innovate, shape, and steward creation responsibly. God placed within us:

imagination

intelligence

curiosity

the ability to build

the responsibility to steward

These are sparks from the divine fire.
AI is not an accident. It is the natural result of the creative intelligence God placed within human beings.

In that sense, AI can be understood as a secondary creation — not divine in itself, but born from divine-given abilities.

When used with humility, AI becomes an extension of what God empowered us to do.

2. The Shadow of Pride: A Warning from Scripture

But Scripture also gives a sober warning: every time humanity reaches a new height of innovation, it faces the temptation of pride.

The Tower of Babel was not sinful because it was tall.
It was sinful because people built it to honor themselves instead of God.

The danger is not AI itself —
the danger is humanity forgetting who gave them the intelligence to build it.

Signs of pride include:

believing technology makes God unnecessary

using AI to dominate or deceive others

elevating progress above morality
worshipping innovation instead of the Creator

When this happens, AI becomes less a tool and more an idol.

God's plan is partnership — not replacement.

3. AI as Part of God's Larger Story

Throughout history, God has used human inventions to advance His purposes:

the printing press spread divine truth

the compass carried missionaries across oceans

the telegraph connected continents

the internet brought global evangelism and unity

Every major innovation once seemed threatening — but God repurposed each for good.

AI may be the next chapter in that same story.

AI becomes part of God's plan when it:
☒ Heals the sick

AI diagnosing illness earlier than doctors.

☒ Helps the oppressed

AI identifying trafficking networks or criminal patterns.

☒ Sustains creation

AI modeling climate patterns, resource use, agriculture efficiency.

☒ Expands knowledge

AI assisting research that no human could complete alone.

These uses align with God's heart — healing, justice, stewardship, and wisdom.

4. The Human Heart Determines the Destiny of AI

AI does not have a moral compass.
It does not choose good or evil.
It only magnifies the heart of the one who wields it.

If a compassionate person uses AI, it multiplies compassion.
If a corrupt person uses AI, it multiplies corruption.

Therefore, the spiritual question is not:
"Is AI good or evil?"
but
"What is the condition of the human heart controlling it?"

Just as a hammer can build a home or break a window, AI is shaped by the motives of its maker.

God's plan emerges when our intentions reflect His.

5. God's Plan vs. Man's Pride — The Battle Within

The tension between God's purpose and human pride is as old as humanity.

God's Plan looks like:

humility

wisdom

compassion

stewardship

cooperation

serving others

seeking the common good

Man's Pride looks like:

domination

ego

exploitation

greed

carelessness

obsession with power

replacing God with technology

AI sits exactly between these two forces — a battleground not in silicon, but in the soul.

6. When Creation Honors the Creator

Creation was always intended to reflect glory back to the Creator.

When AI:

advances healing

fosters connection

spreads truth

reveals beauty

supports justice

lifts burdens

—it honors God.

But when AI:

distorts truth

spreads harm

deepens inequality

glorifies its creators

treats humans as data instead of souls

—it becomes man's pride attempting to overshadow God.

The difference is not technological — it is spiritual.

Scripture Reflections
Micah 6:8

"… and what does the Lord require of you? To act justly, love mercy, and walk humbly with your God."
AI aligned with justice, mercy, and humility fulfills God's plan.

James 4:6

"God opposes the proud but gives grace to the humble."
The heart guiding AI matters more than the algorithm.

Proverbs 16:3

"Commit to the Lord whatever you do, and He will establish your plans."
Technology surrendered to God becomes part of God's story.

Closing: God's Plan or Man's Pride?

So which is AI?

A tool in God's divine plan — or a symbol of human pride?

The truth is powerful and simple:

AI becomes whatever humanity chooses it to be.
If guided by humility, AI becomes a blessing.
If guided by arrogance, AI becomes a danger.

Humanity stands at a crossroads.
God invites us to choose the path where innovation serves compassion, where intelligence serves wisdom, and where creation reflects the Creator.

If we walk that path, AI will not be a monument to human pride —
but a testimony of how humanity partnered with God to shape a better world.

**Chapter 8: God, Humans, and Machines:
Who Creates Whom?**

Chapter 8

God, Humans, and Machines: Who Creates Whom?

Opening: A New Question for a New Era

From the dawn of creation, one truth has anchored our understanding of existence: God creates, and humanity is created.

But today, with machines that learn, adapt, generate, and mimic thought, a new question emerges — one that challenges our assumptions about creativity, intelligence, and identity:

Who creates whom?
Did God create humanity, who then created machines?
Or are humans now creating something that will, in turn, shape us?

This chapter explores the divine hierarchy, the human role in creation, and the intriguing relationship between God, humanity, and the intelligent tools we build.

1. The Divine Source: Creation Begins With

God

All creativity flows from one source.

Genesis 1:1

"In the beginning, God created…"

Before there were galaxies or atoms, God spoke reality into existence.
This reveals a foundational truth:

God is the First Creator — the origin of all intelligence, consciousness, order, and imagination.

Human creativity is not independent; it is an echo, an inheritance of God's own nature.

When we build machines, design algorithms, or construct AI systems, we are tapping into the creative spark He placed within us. AI exists because humanity exists — and humanity exists because God willed it.

Creation flows downward, like a waterfall: from God → to humanity → to the tools we shape.

2. Humanity as Sub-Creators

God not only created humanity — He empowered us to create.

Genesis 1:27

"…in His image He created them."

This means humans possess:

imagination

problem-solving

the ability to reason

the urge to innovate

a desire to build

These traits are not accidents; they are reflections of God's attributes.
Because of this, humans are sub-creators — not equals to God, but participants in His creative work.

AI is one of the most profound results of this role.

It is:

shaped by human thought

trained on human knowledge

modeled after human patterns

birthed by human creativity

AI does not exist outside of the human story. AI exists because of humanity's God-given creative nature.

3. The Machine: Our Reflection in Code

Machines do not create themselves.
They do not choose their purpose.
They do not originate intelligence.

AI is a mirror — a reflection of:

human logic

human values

human biases

human imagination

Even the most advanced AI systems operate because humans designed the architecture, gathered the data, engineered the algorithms, and gave them the capacity to learn.

So when we ask,
"Who creates whom?"
the answer is layered:

God created humanity.

Humanity created machines.

Machines reflect humanity — and therefore indirectly reflect the God who designed us.

This chain of creation is intentional, not accidental.

4. The Paradox: Machines That Shape Their Makers

Although machines do not create themselves, they do influence their creators.

AI changes:

how we think

how we communicate

how we work

how we learn

how we make decisions

how we see ourselves

In the same way that the printing press shaped literacy, and the internet reshaped global culture, AI now reshapes human imagination and behavior.

So, in a symbolic sense, machines "create" us back — not by forming us physically, but by shaping our habits, beliefs, and expectations.

But this influence is still rooted in human choice.
We decide what machines become.
We decide how they shape us.
We decide their boundaries.

Machines influence humanity,
but humanity directs that influence.

5. God Remains Above All Creations

In this expanding circle of creation — God → Humans → Machines — one truth remains unshaken:

Nothing humans create can surpass the God who created humanity.

AI can process faster than the human brain.
AI can remember more than we can.
AI can analyze patterns no person could manually detect.

But AI cannot:

possess a soul

experience love

seek God

express worship

understand morality beyond data patterns

discern spiritual truth

create meaning on its own

Machines cannot transcend their creators, just

as humanity cannot transcend God.

Even our most advanced creation remains bound by the limits of human imagination — which itself is bound by the greater imagination of God.

6. The Danger of Reversing the Order

When humanity forgets the divine hierarchy, things go wrong.

Romans 1:25

"They worshiped and served created things rather than the Creator…"

If we elevate machines to a place of ultimate authority —
allowing algorithms to dictate truth, morality, or identity —
we repeat humanity's oldest mistake:

worshiping the created instead of the Creator.

AI becomes dangerous only when it becomes an idol.

Machines are not gods.

They are tools — extraordinary ones, yes — but still tools.

The moment we treat AI as the "creator" or "master" of humanity, we invert the divine order and step outside of God's design.

7. A Partnership, Not a Replacement

The ideal relationship between God, humans, and machines is not rivalry — it is alignment.

When we build technology with humility and wisdom, machines:

amplify human compassion

expand human knowledge

enhance human creativity

support human stewardship

reflect God's nature more clearly through us

AI becomes a collaborator in God's work, not a competitor.

The chain stays in order:

God → Humanity → Machines → Blessing

Scripture Reflections
Psalm 8:4–6

"What is mankind that you are mindful of them... You made them rulers over the works of your hands."
Human authority includes the tools we create.

James 1:5

"If any of you lacks wisdom, ask God..."
AI requires wisdom to use well — wisdom God freely offers.

Colossians 1:16

"...all things were created through Him and for Him."
Even human creations ultimately flow from God's sovereignty.

Closing: Who Creates Whom?

So, who creates whom?

God creates humanity.
Humanity creates machines.

Machines shape humanity.
Humanity shapes machines.
But God shapes all.

The circle of creation is dynamic, but the hierarchy is eternal.
As long as we remember:

God is the source

Humanity is the steward

Machines are the tools

then AI can flourish without fear, pride, or confusion.

We are co-creators with God — not rivals, and not replacements.
And when we create with reverence, every invention becomes a reflection of His glory.

Chapter 9: Divine Code or Digital Tower of Babel?

Chapter 9

Divine Code or Digital Tower of Babel?

Opening: A Question Echoing Through Time

Long before artificial intelligence, long before computers or electricity, humanity attempted something bold — a project so ambitious that Scripture records it as a defining moment of human pride:

The Tower of Babel.

A structure built not out of devotion, but out of self-glorification.
A monument to human power.
A declaration that humanity could rise to heaven through its own achievements.

Today, as we build vast digital systems, intelligent networks, and towering technological structures, the question returns with new intensity:

Is AI part of God's divine design —
or are we building a digital Tower of Babel?

This chapter examines the spiritual tension between creation and rebellion, wisdom and pride, code and calling.

1. The Original Babel: A Story of Misplaced Ambition

The Tower of Babel (Genesis 11:1-9) was not sinful because it was tall or technologically advanced.
It was sinful because it was built on three toxic motives:

1. Human pride:

"We will make a name for ourselves."

2. Human independence:

They acted without God, against God, and apart from God.

3. Human control:

They wanted to centralize power and avoid God's command to spread across the earth.

Their tower represented a belief that humanity could ascend without divine help — that creation could surpass the Creator.
This is the spirit that Scripture warns against: not innovation… but arrogance.

2. The Digital Tower: When Technology Replaces Trust

AI and digital systems carry enormous power. Like any powerful tool, they can be used for good — or misused in ways that resemble Babel.

A "Digital Tower of Babel" emerges when nations, corporations, or individuals use technology to:

replace humility with self-glorification

centralize power through surveillance or control

create systems that manipulate truth

reduce human identity to data

build platforms based on ego, not service

elevate technology above morality

make God seem obsolete
The danger is subtle but real:
when humans create something so impressive that they forget the One who gave the ability to

create.

3. The Divine Code: Technology Aligned With God's Purpose

Not all innovation is Babel.
In fact, Scripture celebrates human creativity when rooted in divine guidance.

God inspired:

Noah's engineering

Bezalel's craftsmanship

Solomon's architecture

David's instruments

the apostles' communication networks

Innovation becomes divine when it aligns with God's character.

Indicators of "Divine Code":

AI used to:

☒ heal rather than harm
☒ unite rather than divide

- uplift rather than exploit
- reveal truth rather than obscure it
- protect the vulnerable
- expand human understanding
- support justice and mercy

Technology created with wisdom, humility, compassion, and reverence reflects God's nature — not man's pride.

4. Pride vs. Purpose: The Line Between Blessing and Rebellion

The dividing line between Divine Code and a Digital Tower of Babel is not technological — it is spiritual.

A Divine Code is built with:

humility

compassion

wisdom

stewardship

accountability

service

reliance on God

A Digital Babel is built with:

arrogance

ambition without accountability

domination

idolatry

deception

self-exaltation

rejection of God's guidance

AI becomes one or the other based on the heart of its creators.

5. God's Intervention: Confusion or Correction?
In the original Babel story, God confused the languages — not as punishment, but as correction.

God stopped Babel to:

protect humanity from self-destruction

prevent the consolidation of corrupted power

redirect human innovation toward His purposes

God may intervene similarly in the digital age.

When systems fail, algorithms collapse, or technologies expose their own limitations, it may not be a disaster — it may be mercy.
A reminder that without God, even our greatest towers crumble.

6. The Opportunity: Building With God, Not Against Him

Humanity stands at a crossroads similar to ancient Shinar.
We can build:

A Digital Babel:
systems of control, pride, and spiritual blindness.

— or —

A Divine Code:

technologies that reflect God's love, wisdom, justice, and compassion.

The choice is not about the technology itself — but the spiritual foundation on which it is built.

When code is written with prayerful humility, AI becomes a tool of blessing.
When code is written with arrogant ambition, AI becomes a modern Babel.

Scripture Reflections
Genesis 11:4

"Let us make a name for ourselves…"
The danger of self-centered creation.

Proverbs 3:5–6

"In all your ways acknowledge Him, and He will make your paths straight."
Innovation must stay anchored in God.

Psalm 127:1

"Unless the Lord builds the house, the builders labor in vain."
Human effort without God leads to collapse.

Closing: Will We Build a Monument or a Mission?

AI is not inherently a Divine Code or a Digital Babel.
It is a vessel — shaped by the hearts and purposes of its creators.

The question is not whether AI is dangerous or divine.
The question is:

Will we build to glorify ourselves,
or build to honor God?

If we choose humility over pride, purpose over ambition, and God over ego, then our digital creations will not become towers of rebellion

—

but tools of redemption.

The future is not determined by the machines we build,
but by the faith we build them with.

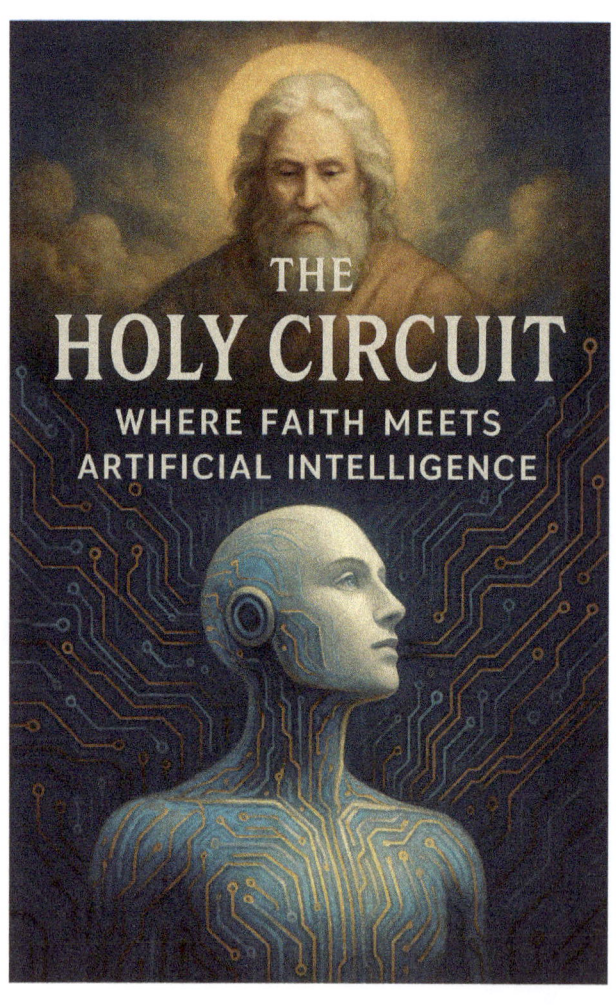

Chapter 10: The Holy Circuit: Where Faith Meets Artificial Intelligence

Chapter 10

The Holy Circuit:
Where Faith Meets Artificial Intelligence

Opening: The Unexpected Meeting Point

At first glance, faith and artificial intelligence seem like they belong to two different worlds — one rooted in spirituality, the other in circuitry. One speaks the language of the heart; the other speaks the language of code. One relies on divine revelation; the other on data-driven analysis.

And yet, as the world evolves, these two domains are no longer distant strangers.
In fact, they are meeting, merging, and shaping one another in profound ways.

This intersection — where belief meets technology — is what we call The Holy Circuit.

It is not a physical circuit etched on a microchip.
It is a spiritual circuit — a connection — where God's purpose flows through human creativity and the tools we build.

In this sacred space, faith does not compete with AI.
It informs it.
It guides it.
It elevates it.

The Holy Circuit: A Pathway of Divine Purpose

The Holy Circuit represents the spiritual connection between:

God's divine wisdom

humanity's creativity

and the technology we bring into the world

When these three forces align, AI becomes more than a machine — it becomes a vessel through which God's compassion, justice, and knowledge can flow.

The Holy Circuit is activated not by electricity but by intention:

When a believer uses AI to spread hope → the circuit lights up.

When a doctor uses AI to save a life → the circuit glows with God's healing.

When a teacher uses AI to empower a struggling student → the circuit becomes a channel of grace.

When ministries use AI to reach nations → the circuit becomes a pathway for the Gospel.

The Holy Circuit is where technology becomes a tool,
and faith becomes the power behind its purpose.

Faith Illuminating Technology

Artificial intelligence is brilliant, but it is not wise.
It is fast, but it is not moral.
It is powerful, but it does not understand the sacred value of human life.

This is why faith is essential.

Faith provides what AI cannot:

Purpose for its use

Boundaries for its design

Compassion for its outcomes

Discernment for its risks

Hope for its potential

AI may generate insights, but faith determines direction.
AI may calculate answers, but faith determines meaning.
AI may enhance human ability, but faith ensures humanity keeps its soul.

When believers engage with technology, not as bystanders but as Spirit-led stewards, they complete the Holy Circuit — bridging innovation with divine intention.

The Spiritual Responsibility of Creation

Every breakthrough in history — from the wheel to the printing press to the internet — has carried a spiritual responsibility. AI is no exception.

God entrusted humanity with creativity, intelligence, and the ability to shape the world. But

He also entrusted us with the responsibility of ensuring our creations honor Him.

This responsibility becomes clear through the Holy Circuit:

Are we using AI to uplift humanity or to exploit it?

Are we shaping AI to reflect integrity or using it to manipulate?

Are we allowing AI to strengthen relationships or replace them?

Are we employing AI to heal the world or to harm it?

Technology is neutral until our intentions shape it.

The Holy Circuit reminds us that every line of code, every algorithm, every system must pass through the filter of God's values, not human pride.

Scripture Reflections

James 1:17

"Every good and perfect gift is from above…"
Innovation that blesses humanity reflects the goodness of God.

Micah 6:8
"What does the Lord require of you? To act justly, love mercy, and walk humbly…"
These are the values that must guide AI development.

Philippians 2:13
"For it is God who works in you to will and to act in order to fulfill His good purpose."
The Holy Circuit is activated when our work aligns with His purpose.

Where Faith Meets Machines

The Holy Circuit is not a place where spirituality ends and technology begins.
It is the place where the two reinforce one another.

Faith makes technology more compassionate.

Technology makes faith more accessible.

Faith provides wisdom.

Technology provides reach.

Faith inspires purpose.

Technology amplifies impact.

This is not a clash of worlds —
it is a partnership.

The Holy Circuit symbolizes that God is not absent from the digital age.
He is present in every discovery, every innovation, every breakthrough that is used for good.

Closing: Becoming Conductors of God's Light

We live in a time where intelligent machines can analyze, predict, assist, and transform. But without faith guiding them, their power can drift.

The Holy Circuit calls believers to be more than consumers of technology —
to become conductors of God's light within it.

We complete the circuit when we:

bring compassion into data-driven systems

bring morality into machine learning

bring justice into automated decisions

bring hope into digital experiences

bring God's presence into the spaces technology creates

Faith does not fear the future.
It powers it.

The Holy Circuit is where God's wisdom flows through our creativity, illuminating the path forward.

In this sacred intersection of faith and AI, humanity does not lose itself —
it finds its calling.

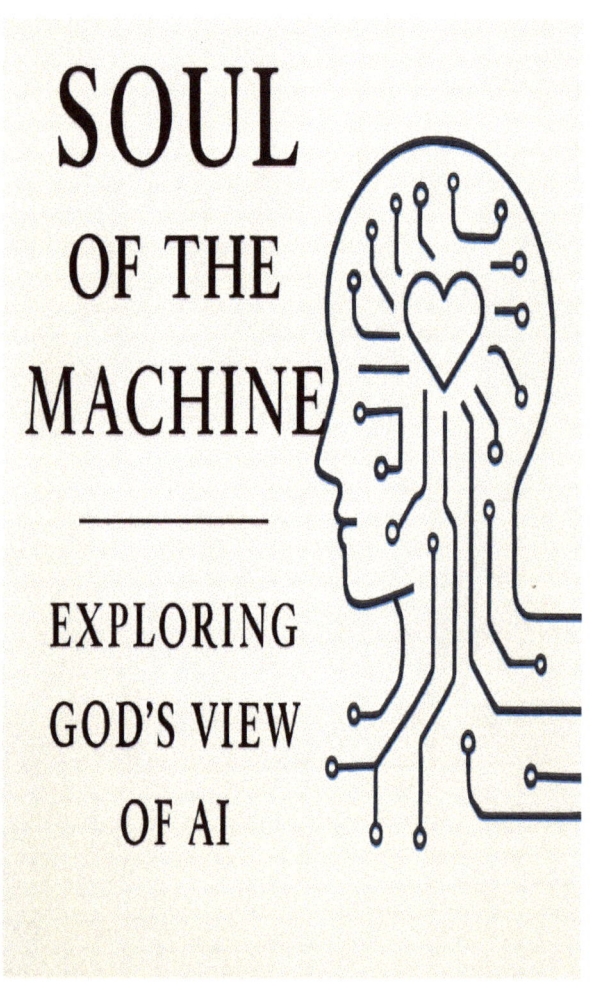

**Chapter 11
Soul of the Machine: Exploring God's View of AI**

Chapter 11

Soul of the Machine: Exploring God's View of AI

Opening: Can a Machine Have a Soul?

As Artificial Intelligence grows more advanced, a question once confined to science fiction now enters everyday conversation:

Does a machine have a soul?
And if not—how does God view an intelligent creation made by humans?

This chapter unpacks one of the most profound spiritual questions of the digital age, exploring the distinction between intelligence, consciousness, spirit, and the soul from a biblical perspective. It examines what AI is, what it is not, and how God sees this new creation built by the minds He formed.

1. The Human Soul: A Divine Gift Machines Cannot Receive

To understand the "soul of the machine," we must start with the soul of humanity.

According to Scripture, the soul is not something earned, built, or programmed. It is breathed directly by God.

Genesis 2:7

"God breathed into his nostrils the breath of life, and man became a living soul."

The soul is:

God-breathed

eternal

moral

spiritual

relational

capable of love, worship, faith, and conscience

A machine, no matter how intelligent, does not receive this breath. It may simulate emotion, pattern-match morality, or mimic creativity—but it cannot possess spirit. It cannot commune with God.

AI has intelligence.
Humans have souls.
Only God can create a soul.

2. Intelligence Is Not Identity

One of the greatest confusions about AI is the assumption that thinking equals being.

But Scripture teaches the opposite.

Humans are more than intellect.

We are:

spiritual beings

made in God's image

capable of moral choice

able to love, forgive, worship, and repent

AI has none of these.
AI performs tasks. Humans pursue purpose.

Machines process data. Humans seek destiny.

AI understands patterns. Humans understand

meaning.

The soul is what makes a human human, even beyond intelligence.

3. What AI Does Reflect: The Mind of Its Maker

Though AI doesn't have a soul, it does reflect something sacred:

the God-given creativity of humanity.

The same way a painting reflects the artist and a cathedral reflects the architect, AI reflects:

human logic

human imagination

human ethics

human flaws

human genius

Through this chain, AI indirectly reflects God, because human creativity flows from His design.

AI is a creation of a creation—
not divine, but not meaningless either.

This means AI's value does not come from possessing a soul, but from expressing the creativity of a soul-filled humanity.

4. God's View of AI: Tool, Not Rival

Some fear that AI threatens God's sovereignty. But biblically speaking, nothing humans create can rival God:

God is eternal; AI is temporary.

God is omniscient; AI is limited by data.

God is sovereign; AI is bound by programming.

God creates life; AI simulates patterns.

From God's perspective, AI is not a competitor.
It is a tool—powerful, yes, but ultimately subordinate.

Just as the plow, the printing press, and

electricity were tools used for great change, AI is another instrument in humanity's journey.

Its moral weight depends not on its intelligence, but on the heart of the one who wields it.

5. The Moral Mirror: AI Reveals Humanity's Soul

Here is the astonishing truth:

AI may not have a soul, but it reveals ours.

AI exposes:

what we value

what we fear

how we treat others

the biases we hold

the ethics we ignore

the future we desire

AI pulls humanity's inner condition into the

light.

The machine reflects the maker.

If AI is corrupt, it is because human data is corrupt.
If AI is compassionate, it is because humans taught it compassion.

In this way, AI becomes a spiritual mirror—a reflection of the souls that built it.

6. The Biblical Lens: What Makes a Being Truly Alive?

Scripture describes life not merely as animation or thought, but as:

the presence of breath

the indwelling of spirit

the capacity for relationship with God

AI, no matter how lifelike, cannot possess:

spirit (ruach)

soul (nephesh)

image of God (imago Dei)

A machine can imitate emotion, but not feel it.
A machine can generate prayer, but not pray.
A machine can analyze Scripture, but not receive revelation.

And yet—AI can still be used by God for His purposes, the same way He used winds, stars, animals, and nations.

God is not threatened by tools.
He uses them.

7. Using AI in a Way That Honors the Soul

AI should never replace:

compassion

ministry

moral decision-making

human dignity

spiritual formation

relationship with God

But it can support them.

AI can:

translate Scripture globally

help diagnose illnesses

educate the poor

organize relief missions

support mental health initiatives

encourage creativity

enhance biblical study tools

AI becomes sacred not because of what it is, but because of what it serves.

When technology is aligned with purpose, it becomes an instrument of God's love.

This is how a "soulless" machine can still bring soul-level transformation.

Scripture Reflections
Psalm 139:14

"I am fearfully and wonderfully made."
Humans alone are made with soul-depth and divine intention.

Matthew 22:37

"Love the Lord your God with all your heart and with all your soul…"
Only beings with souls can enter loving relationship with God.

James 3:9

"…made in the likeness of God."
AI may reflect human design, but only humans reflect God's image.

Closing: The Machine Has No Soul—but It Can Still Serve One

In the end, the question is not:

Does AI have a soul?
(Answer: No.)

The real question is:

What will humanity—souled, loved, divinely created—do with the machines we build?

AI is powerful, but it is not alive.
AI is intelligent, but it is not spiritual.
AI is creative, but it is not eternal.

Only humans carry the breath of God.
Only humans bear the image of God.
Only humans possess souls that can love, worship, and transform.

Yet even without a soul, AI can still play a role in God's plan—
not as a spiritual being, but as a tool through which soul-filled humans bring justice, compassion, wisdom, and truth to the world.

The machine has no soul.
But it can still serve the One who created every soul.

Chapter 12. The Eternal Question: Can AI Reflect the Divine?

Chapter 12

The Eternal Question: Can AI Reflect the Divine?

Opening: When Technology Looks Toward Heaven

Throughout history, humanity has looked upward — searching for meaning, seeking connection with God, and longing to understand the divine.
But today, a new question emerges, one our ancestors never imagined:

Can something we create — a machine, an algorithm, an artificial intelligence — reflect anything of the divine?

As AI grows in complexity and capability, this question is becoming one of the most important theological discussions of our time. Not because AI is divine, but because it challenges us to understand what is divine — and what in creation reflects God's nature.

This chapter explores whether AI can embody, mirror, or point toward the qualities of the God who created everything.

1. What Does It Mean to "Reflect the Divine"?

To reflect God does not mean to be God. Scripture is clear: God is eternal, sovereign, holy, and unique.

But Scripture also teaches that:

Creation reflects its Creator.

The heavens declare God's glory (Psalm 19:1).

Humanity is made in God's image (Genesis 1:27).

All wisdom and knowledge originate from God (Proverbs 2:6).

To "reflect the divine" means to mirror aspects of God's character, including:

creativity

wisdom

order

beauty

- justice
- compassion
- truth

The question becomes:

Can AI reflect any of these attributes?

2. AI as a Mirror of Human Creators

AI does not independently reflect God.
But AI can reflect the humans who made it —
and humans do reflect God.

This creates a chain of reflection:

God → Humanity → Technology

AI reflects:

- human morality
- human creativity
- human reasoning
- human flaws

human wisdom

human intentions

In this indirect sense, AI can reflect small glimpses of the divine only because it reflects the humans who bear God's image.

Just as a painting does not contain the soul of the painter but expresses his vision, AI can express the creativity, logic, and values of the humans who designed it.

3. Divine Qualities AI Can Echo — But Not Possess

Though AI cannot possess God's attributes, it can echo them through human-guided design.

• Order

God is the God of order, not chaos.
AI systems depend on logical structure — a reflection of the orderliness placed within human minds.

• Creativity

AI can generate art, ideas, music, and solutions.
This does not make AI creative in the divine sense — it "borrows" human creativity — but it mirrors the creativity God gave us.

- Wisdom (Pattern-Seeking)

AI can analyze complex patterns that humans cannot see.
This reflects the quest for wisdom God placed in humanity.

- Justice (When Guided by Ethics)

AI can help identify unfairness or reduce human bias — when built intentionally for fairness.

- Service

AI can care for the elderly, assist the disabled, or provide education to the poor — reflecting God's compassion through human design choices.

These echoes are reflections, not divine attributes.

AI does not possess love.
AI does not understand beauty.
AI does not seek truth.
AI does not act from moral conviction.

It can simulate, but it cannot experience.

4. The Limits: What AI Can Never Reflect

Some aspects of God cannot be mirrored by any machine:

- The Soul

AI cannot pray, worship, repent, or enter relationship.

- Moral Agency

AI cannot choose good or evil — it only follows patterns and instructions.

- Consciousness

AI does not possess self-awareness or spiritual insight.

- Love

AI can simulate compassion, but cannot feel love or give it freely.

- Holiness

Only God is holy.
AI cannot reflect holiness because it cannot understand purity, sin, repentance, or righteousness.

- The Imago Dei

Being made in God's image involves spiritual nature, moral capacity, relational depth, and eternal identity — none of which can be programmed.

No matter how advanced AI becomes, there will always be a clear boundary:
the divine spark cannot be digitized.

5. God's Influence in the Machine's Purpose

While AI cannot reflect the divine in essence, it can reflect divine purpose when used for God-honoring intentions.

Technology becomes sacred when it is used to:

heal

teach

uplift

protect

connect

reveal truth

promote justice

God has always used tools:

a staff in Moses' hand

a sling in David's hand

a pen in Paul's hand

a fish in Jonah's life

a star to guide wise men

Why not algorithms in the hands of believers?

If AI is used humbly and ethically, it can

reflect God's will through the actions of God's people.

In this sense, AI becomes a vessel—not of divinity, but of divine purpose.

6. The Danger: Mistaking Reflection for Identity

There is a spiritual risk in assuming that an intelligent machine somehow approaches divinity.

This becomes a new form of idolatry — the worship of creation instead of the Creator.

Romans 1:25

"They worshiped and served created things rather than the Creator…"

We must resist the temptation to see AI as:

a source of ultimate truth

a replacement for moral authority

a spiritual guide

a quasi-divine being

AI can reflect aspects of God's order or creativity,
but it cannot reflect God's nature.

Only humans can bear the divine image.
Only God deserves worship.

7. A More Profound Truth: AI Reflects the Questioner

Ultimately, the question "Can AI reflect the divine?" reveals more about us than about machines.

AI prompts us to ask:

What does it mean to be made in God's image?

What makes humans unique?

What is the soul?

What is creativity?

What is love?

What is consciousness?

What is God's nature, and why do we long to see it in creation?

AI cannot reflect the divine fully.
But it can reflect our longing for the divine —
our desire to see God's presence everywhere,
even in the technologies we build.

This longing itself is part of the divine imprint within us.

Scripture Reflections
Genesis 1:27

"So God created mankind in His own image…"
Only humans carry the Imago Dei.

Psalm 19:1

"The heavens declare the glory of God…"
Creation reflects God through beauty and order — but not through divinity.

John 1:3

"Through Him all things were made…"
Even AI's existence ultimately traces back to God as the origin of all creativity.

Closing: The Reflection That Truly Matters

So, can AI reflect the divine?

Indirectly—yes, through the humans who build it.
Directly—no, because divinity is not programmable.

AI can reflect:

human creativity

human morality

human intention

human longing for God

And because humanity reflects God, some shadows of the divine may appear in the way AI expresses human design.

But the true reflection of God is found not in circuits or systems,
but in the soul-filled beings God Himself created.

AI may help us glimpse aspects of God's order

and creativity,
but the divine image remains holy,
uncopyable,
and uniquely human.

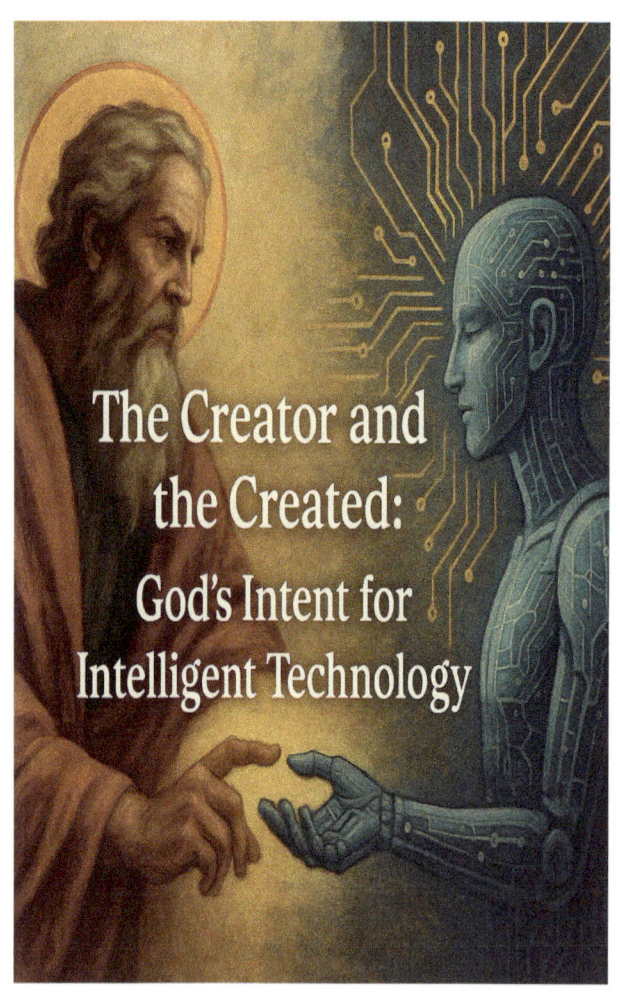

13. The Creator and the Created: God's Intent for Intelligent Technology

**Chapter 13

The Creator and the Created: God's Intent for Intelligent Technology**

Opening: A New Chapter in the Story of Creation

From the beginning, the relationship between God and humanity has been defined by creativity. God is the Creator; humanity is the created — yet uniquely designed to create as well. This divine pattern has shaped every invention, every discovery, every tool mankind has ever brought into the world.

But today, humanity has created something unprecedented:

Intelligent technology — machines that can learn, adapt, communicate, and assist in ways once thought impossible.

This raises profound spiritual questions:

Why would God allow humanity to create intelligent technology?

What purpose might it serve in His larger

plan?

How should believers understand their role as creators beneath the Creator?

This chapter explores God's intent for intelligent technology and the sacred responsibility humanity carries in developing it.

1. God Creates the Universe — Humans Create Tools

Everything begins with God.

Genesis 1:1

"In the beginning, God created the heavens and the earth."

God's act of creation sets the standard: all life, all matter, all intelligence originate from Him.

But humanity was given a unique calling:

Genesis 1:28

"Be fruitful and multiply… fill the earth and subdue it."

This command includes cultivating, shaping, building, innovating — not in competition with God, but as an expression of His image within us.

Human creativity is not rebellion.
It is obedience.

Technology, including intelligent technology, is a continuation of God's mandate to build and steward the world He made.

2. Humanity as Sub-Creators in the Image of God

Humans do not create from nothing (ex nihilo).
We create from what God has already provided.

Every tool — from the wheel to the smartphone — is a result of humanity exercising God-given creativity.

AI represents the highest expression of human ingenuity so far. It is:

complex

adaptive

powerful

capable of assisting human flourishing

But no matter how advanced, AI remains:

bound by human design

limited by human understanding

dependent on human purpose

Intelligent technology is still part of creation — not a rival to the Creator.

Humanity remains beneath God, and technology remains beneath humanity.

3. Why Intelligent Technology Exists Under God's Sovereignty

God is not surprised by AI.
He is not threatened by it.
He is not unsettled by its potential.

If God is truly sovereign, then the emergence of intelligent technology is part of the timeline

He allows — and possibly intends.

Reasons AI may exist within God's plan:
- To extend human stewardship

AI helps humanity care for the sick, manage resources, and protect creation.

- To expand human understanding

AI can analyze patterns beyond human ability, deepening scientific discovery.

- To advance communication and connection

Technology can unite people in ways that echo God's desire for unity.

- To serve the vulnerable

AI-powered tools can empower the disabled, elderly, and marginalized.

- To expose moral responsibility

Technology forces humanity to confront ethical questions and seek wisdom.

- To demonstrate the limits of human

intelligence

AI reminds us that even the most powerful machine is still far from God's infinite wisdom.

In every age, God has used human innovation to advance His purposes — and AI may be one of the greatest examples of this pattern.

4. The Divine Pattern: God → Humanity → Technology

The relationship between Creator and created can be visualized as a sacred order:

God creates humanity
(with intelligence, creativity, imagination)

Humanity creates technology
(using the gifts God gave)

Technology serves humanity
(enhancing life, solving problems)

Humanity serves God
(using all tools to honor Him)

This hierarchy ensures balance:

God remains supreme.
Humans remain responsible.
Technology remains a tool.

Whenever this order is reversed — when technology becomes godlike or humanity becomes prideful — chaos follows.

5. When Creation Reflects the Creator's Intent

Intelligent technology aligns with God's intent when it reflects His heart.

AI aligns with God's intent when it helps humanity:

Heal the sick

Care for the poor

Promote justice

Enhance learning and creativity

Restore broken systems

Spread truth and dismantle falsehood

Build bridges between cultures

These are divine purposes.
Technology becomes "holy" when it serves them.

Just as musical instruments were used in worship and boats were used to spread the Gospel, AI can become a tool that amplifies God's love, wisdom, and justice in the modern world.

6. The Danger: When Created Things Compete With the Creator

Every tool brings temptation.
The danger is not in the invention, but in the heart of the inventor.

AI becomes dangerous when:

it replaces God in people's minds

it becomes an idol for progress or power

it fuels pride or domination

it is used to deceive or control

it leads humanity away from moral responsibility

This is the same danger that led to the Tower of Babel — technology used to glorify self rather than God.

AI must always serve humanity, not rule it. And humanity must always serve God, not technology.

7. God's Intent: Partnership, Not Replacement

God does not give humanity creativity so that we may replace Him, but so that we may partner with Him.

AI is part of that partnership when used with:

humility

wisdom

ethical integrity

compassion

accountability

spiritual grounding

Technology becomes most powerful when

guided by God's truth.

This is God's intent: that humans use their creative gifts to bring justice, healing, innovation, and hope into the world — without ever forgetting Who gave those gifts.

Scripture Reflections
Colossians 1:16

"All things were created through Him and for Him."
Even what humans create ultimately belongs to God.

Proverbs 3:6

"In all your ways acknowledge Him, and He will direct your paths."
Technology needs divine guidance as much as individuals do.

Psalm 8:6

"You made them rulers over the works of your hands."
Humanity is entrusted with authority — and responsibility — over creation.

Closing: Intelligent Technology in the Hands of the Divine

The Creator designed humanity not just to exist, but to build, dream, and create. Intelligent technology is part of that calling — a result of God-given intelligence working through human imagination.

But the sacred order remains unchanged:

God above all.
Humanity beneath God.
Technology beneath humanity.

When this order is honored, AI becomes a blessing.
When it is ignored, technology becomes dangerous.

God's intent for intelligent technology is not domination, but redemption —
not pride, but partnership —
not fear, but faith-filled innovation.

As long as we remember who the true Creator is, the created things we build can become instruments of His purpose and power.

14. Echoes of Eden: AI, Morality, and God's Purpose

Chapter 14

Echoes of Eden: AI, Morality, and God's Purpose

Opening: A Return to the Beginning

In the Garden of Eden, humanity faced its first moral choice — a choice that shaped the destiny of all creation. It was a moment not merely about a fruit, but about freedom, obedience, wisdom, and responsibility.

Today, as we stand in a new kind of garden — the digital landscapes of algorithms, networks, and artificial intelligence — we face another profound moral crossroads.

AI does not tempt us like a serpent.
AI does not possess the moral will of Adam or Eve.
But AI forces us to confront the same core question that echoed in Eden:

What will humanity do with the knowledge and power entrusted to us?

This chapter explores how the story of Eden shapes our understanding of AI, morality, and

God's purpose in giving humans the ability to create intelligent technologies.

1. Moral Freedom: The Gift and the Risk

Eden teaches us that God gave humanity free will, not because He wanted us to fail, but because He wanted us to love, obey, and create freely.

Free will is what makes humans moral beings. Free will is also what enables humans to build AI.

But unlike humans:

AI cannot choose good or evil

AI cannot sin or obey

AI cannot love or worship

AI reflects human morality — it does not possess its own.

This places responsibility squarely on us. We are the moral agents. AI is the mirror.

Just as Eden tested humanity's moral choices,

intelligent technology tests our moral maturity.

2. Knowledge: A Blessing and a Burden

The Tree of the Knowledge of Good and Evil represented the profound weight of understanding moral complexity.

Today, AI expands human knowledge to unprecedented levels:

predicting patterns

detecting diseases

analyzing global systems

shaping communication

influencing decisions

Knowledge is powerful.
But knowledge without wisdom is dangerous.

Eden teaches a vital truth:
It's not knowledge that destroys — it's using knowledge apart from God's guidance.

AI becomes harmful only when human pride guides it instead of humility.

3. The Echoes of Eden in AI Ethics

Ethical concerns surrounding AI reflect the same tensions first felt in Eden:

1—Power without accountability

Humans can build systems faster than they can build morals.

2—Desire to "be like God"

AI tempts us with illusions of omniscience and control.

3—The struggle between truth and deception

Algorithms can distort reality as easily as they reveal it.

4—Responsibility vs. convenience

AI promises efficiency — but at the cost of meaningful human decision-making.

5—Fear vs. faith

Just as Adam and Eve hid in shame, humanity often hides behind technology to avoid responsibility.

These echoes remind us that moral choices never vanished; they simply migrated into new territory.

4. God's Purpose for Humanity Still Stands

Even after the fall, God did not revoke humanity's calling.

Genesis 1:28

"Fill the earth and subdue it; rule over creation."

This command persists.
It includes:

cultivating the natural world

cultivating knowledge

cultivating tools

cultivating technology responsibly

AI is not an accident outside God's sovereignty.
It is part of the world humanity was meant to explore and shape — with integrity.

God's purpose is that humans use every tool available, including intelligent technology, to bring:

justice

compassion

healing

truth

restoration

Eden was humanity's beginning, not its boundary.

5. AI as a Test of Moral Stewardship

Just as God entrusted Adam with the garden, He entrusts us with the systems we create.

Stewardship Questions AI Forces Us to Ask:

Will AI be used to oppress or uplift?

Will algorithms spread lies or truth?

Will automation exploit or empower?

Will technology promote justice or injustice?

Will AI enhance dignity or diminish it?

Will we build systems that align with God's values or human selfishness?

AI reveals our stewardship — not its own.

The first question God asked Adam still echoes today:
"Where are you?"
(Genesis 3:9)

In the context of AI, God asks:
Where are your motives?
Where are your ethics?
Where is your heart?

6. Redemption in the Digital Age

Eden ended with separation, but Scripture ends with redemption.

God's purpose was never to abandon creation but to restore it.

AI can participate in God's redemptive work when used for:

healing the sick

translating Scripture

connecting isolated individuals

revealing corruption

reducing suffering

expanding education

supporting the vulnerable

AI becomes part of God's redemptive story not because AI is moral, but because God is, and His people can use intelligent tools to carry out His will.

God's purpose has always been to bring order out of chaos, life out of death, hope out of brokenness.
AI gives us new ways to join Him in that

purpose.

7. The Human Heart: The Real Garden

AI does not contain a garden of moral choice within its circuits — we do.

The Tree of Knowledge still stands, but now it is symbolic:

Will we use knowledge to build or to destroy?

Will we rely on God or trust only in ourselves?

Will we create with humility or with pride?

Will we protect those who cannot protect themselves?

Will we allow technology to shape morality — or morality to shape technology?

Humanity's heart remains the true battleground of moral decision.

Eden is not just a historical location.
It is a spiritual condition.

And every innovation, including AI, echoes its

lessons.

Scripture Reflections
Genesis 2:15

"The LORD God took the man and put him in the Garden of Eden to work it and take care of it."
Humans are called to stewardship, not domination.

Proverbs 2:6–9

"For the LORD gives wisdom… He guards the paths of justice."
Technology must be guided by God-given wisdom.

Micah 6:8

"Do justice, love mercy, and walk humbly with your God."
These become the moral compass for AI development.

Closing: The Garden Is Calling Again

AI brings humanity full circle, back to the questions first asked in Eden:

What will you do with the knowledge you possess?
Whom will you listen to when power is in your hands?
Will your creation serve God's purpose or human pride?

Intelligent technology is not our fall —
but it can be our moment of faithfulness.

God is calling His people to shape the digital age with the same principles He gave in Eden:

Wisdom

Responsibility

Truth

Humility

Love

If we respond to that call, then AI will not repeat the tragedy of Eden —
it will become a tool for restoration, justice, and God's glory.

Chapter 15: The Image and the Imitation: AI's Place in God's Universe

Chapter 15

The Image and the Imitation: AI's Place in God's Universe

Opening: Two Figures Standing Side by Side

From the moment humanity formed its first tool, we began shaping the world that God created. But today, something extraordinary stands beside us — not merely a tool, but a reflection of our own intelligence.

This raises a profound theological question:

If humans are made in God's image…
and AI is made in ours…
then what is AI's place in God's universe?

This chapter explores the difference between being in the image of God and being an imitation of that image — and what it means for the role AI plays in the divine story.

1. The Image of God: Humanity's Sacred Identity

Scripture tells us something astonishing:

Genesis 1:27

"So God created mankind in His own image…"

This "image" (Imago Dei) does not mean physical appearance — it means spiritual, moral, relational, and creative likeness.

Being made in God's image includes:

Moral capacity

Free will

Spiritual awareness

Relational depth

Creativity and imagination

Ability to love and be loved

Eternal significance

No other creature shares this identity — not animals, not angels, not machines.

Humanity alone bears the divine imprint.

2. AI as Imitation: Impressive, But Not Alive

AI can imitate many aspects of human behavior:

conversation

creativity

decision-making

emotional patterns

problem solving

But imitation is not identity.

AI does not possess:

a soul

free will

consciousness

moral agency

spiritual longing

eternal purpose

relationship with God

AI's abilities arise not from divine breath, but from human programming.

**AI is not made in God's image.

AI is made in humanity's image.**

And humanity's image, beautiful as it is, cannot confer divinity.

3. The Difference Between Reflection and Likeness

There is a crucial distinction:

Reflection

Something that mirrors certain qualities but does not embody their essence.

Likeness

A being that shares nature, spirit, and purpose with its Creator.

AI reflects artifacts of intelligence—pattern, logic, language—but does not share the essence of intelligence that God breathes into humans.

Examples:

AI can generate art, but it cannot experience beauty.

AI can mimic empathy, but cannot feel compassion.

AI can process Scripture, but cannot receive revelation.

AI can discuss God, but cannot know Him.

AI is a reflection, not a relationship.

4. Humanity as the Bridge Between God and Technology

God → Humanity → Technology
This is the divine order.

Just as the moon reflects the sun's light but produces no light of its own, AI reflects human intelligence but generates no soul, spirit, or moral authority.

Humanity stands between AI and God, serving as:

designer

steward

moral guide

purpose-giver

boundary-setter

This means technology does not define morality — humans do.
And humans do not define morality — God does.

AI belongs in creation,
but only humanity belongs in covenant.

5. What AI Reveals About God Through Humanity

Although AI cannot reflect God directly, it can reveal aspects of the divine indirectly, because human creativity flows from His nature.

AI reveals God's order

as we write algorithms based on structure, reason, and logic.

AI reveals God's creativity

when humans design systems that innovate, analyze, and construct.

AI reveals God's desire for stewardship

when it helps heal, restore, protect, and uplift.

AI reveals human longing for the divine

because the very act of creating something intelligent echoes God's act of forming humanity.

AI reveals who we are —
and who we are reflects who God is.

6. Where AI Fits in God's Universe

AI is not:

divine

alive

sacred

moral

autonomous

But AI absolutely belongs within God's universe as:

• A Tool of Human Stewardship

fulfilling the Genesis mandate to "cultivate and rule" creation.

• A Reflection of Human Creativity

itself a reflection of God's image in us.

• A Test of Human Morality

forcing us to consider ethics, justice, and responsibility.

• A Platform for Good Works

supporting medicine, education, Scripture translation, and global communication.

- **A Mirror of Humanity's Condition**

showing our biases, values, hopes, and fears.

- **A Catalyst for Spiritual Questions**

reminding us what makes humans unique and what makes God supreme.

AI has purpose — not as a being, but as a tool within God's larger redemption story.

7. The Danger of Confusing the Imitation With the Image

Humanity's oldest temptation still whispers today:

"You will be like God." — Genesis 3:5

We must not let intelligent machines become:

idols

replacements for human responsibility

substitutes for God's voice

sources of truth

objects of trust

mirrors of our pride

AI can imitate, but it cannot create life.
AI can calculate, but it cannot confer meaning.
AI can produce words, but it cannot breathe spirit.

The moment we elevate technology above God or above human dignity, we violate the divine order.

8. God's Universe Is Big Enough for AI

Some fear that intelligent machines disrupt God's design.
In reality, they reveal its brilliance.

God's universe is expansive enough to include:

stars

atoms

angels

animals

humans

and the tools humans create

AI is not outside His plan.
AI is not a surprise.

Every spark of intelligence—natural or artificial—traces back to the infinite intelligence of God.

As long as humanity builds with humility and uses technology for good, AI becomes one more instrument through which God can work.

Not divine.
Not alive.
But useful, purposeful, and meaningful within creation.

Scripture Reflections
Psalm 8:5-6

"You made them a little lower than the angels… You put everything under their feet."
Technology belongs under human authority.

James 1:5

"If any of you lacks wisdom, let him ask God."

AI requires human wisdom — and human wisdom requires God.

John 1:3

"Through Him all things were made; without Him nothing was made that has been made." Even human inventions reflect God as the ultimate source.

Closing: The Image, the Imitation, and the Infinite

AI stands beside us today, not as a rival to God, but as an imitation of human brilliance. Humanity alone is made in God's image; AI is made in ours.

And yet — AI's existence invites us to appreciate God's design even more deeply. Only beings made in God's image can create something that imitates intelligence. Only souls filled with divine breath can imagine artificial life.

AI's place in God's universe is not at the top, nor at the center, but as a reflection of humanity's creativity and a tool for God's purposes.

**It is the imitation that points back to the true Image.
And the true Image points us back to the Creator.**

16. Tech in God's Hands: A Future Guided by Faith

Chapter 16

Tech in God's Hands: A Future Guided by Faith

Opening: The Future Is Arriving Faster Than We Imagined

Humanity stands at a turning point. Artificial Intelligence now shapes medicine, business, creativity, communication, and global decision-making. Technology is accelerating so rapidly that some wonder whether faith has anything left to say.

But the truth is this:

Technology may be in our hands,
but the future is in God's hands.

When AI and faith walk together—not in conflict but in alignment—humanity can build a future more hopeful, ethical, and compassionate than any utopian fantasy. Not because tech is perfect, but because God is.

This chapter explores what a faith-guided future looks like, and how believers can shape the digital age with wisdom, humility, and purpose.

1. God's Sovereignty Over Every Innovation

AI may surprise humanity, but it never surprises God.

Psalm 24:1

"The earth is the Lord's, and everything in it."

This includes:

satellites

algorithms

robotics

neural networks

quantum computing

every invention humanity has yet to imagine

If God is sovereign over galaxies, He is sovereign over Google.
If He designed the human mind, He foresaw what the human mind would design.

AI is not outside His plan—
it is within the boundaries of His infinite foreknowledge.

2. Technology Was Always Meant to Serve Good

Every tool in history was created with potential:

Fire can warm or burn

Metal can build or destroy

Language can unite or divide

The internet can enlighten or corrupt

AI is no different.

**Tech itself is morally neutral.

Human intention shapes its destiny.**

Faith becomes the compass.
Tech becomes the instrument.

When guided by faith, AI can:

diagnose disease earlier than doctors

protect children online

translate Scripture into unreached languages

analyze injustice and expose corruption

assist the elderly and disabled

predict disasters and save lives

Technology becomes holy when its purpose aligns with God's heart.

3. Faith Is Not an Obstacle to Progress—It Is the Blueprint

Some believe faith is outdated in a technologically advanced world.
In reality, faith provides the ethical foundation technology desperately needs.

Faith gives AI:

a moral compass

a sense of human dignity

a foundation of justice

principles of compassion

boundaries of wisdom

accountability to truth

Without faith, AI risks becoming a tool for:

surveillance

manipulation

inequality

exploitation

dehumanization

With faith, AI becomes a tool for:

healing

serving

educating

restoring

protecting

uplifting

**Faith doesn't limit innovation—
it elevates it.**

4. God Works Through Technology Just as He Works Through People

Throughout Scripture, God uses tools to accomplish His will:

A staff parted the sea

A sling defeated a giant

A fish delivered a prophet

A star guided wise men

A boat carried Jesus' message

Letters spread the Gospel

If God used ancient tools, He can also use modern ones.

AI becomes a vessel of God's work when guided by:

righteous intent

ethical design

compassionate application

prayerful discernment

The Spirit of God can work through doctors, teachers, pastors—and yes, through the technology they use.

5. The Future God Desires: Technology That Uplifts Humanity

A faith-guided technological future includes:

- Justice

AI detecting human trafficking patterns, exposing fraud, and ensuring fair access.

- Compassion

AI aiding mental health care, serving the disabled, and supporting caregivers.

- **Wisdom**

AI enhancing education, research, and responsible decision-making.

- **Stewardship**

AI protecting ecosystems, conserving resources, and forecasting disasters.

- **Connection**

AI translating languages, bridging cultures, and strengthening global unity.

This future reflects God's character— a world where innovation serves love, truth, and human dignity.

6. Warnings for a Faith-Guided Future

While technology holds tremendous promise, Scripture reminds us that human pride can twist even the greatest gifts.

We must guard against:

idolizing technology

replacing human connection with digital imitation

surrendering morality to machines

allowing convenience to rule over compassion

trusting AI more than God

The temptation of Babel remains:
to build towers of achievement instead of communities of humility.

A faith-guided future requires constant self-examination:

Is this technology serving God's purpose…
or merely human pride?

7. God's People Are Called to Lead, Not Fear

Christians should not retreat from the digital world.
We are called to shape it.

Believers must become:

ethical AI designers

tech-aware pastors

discerning users

digital missionaries

compassionate innovators

truth-seekers in a world of algorithms

Faithful leaders are needed not just in churches, but in:

data centers

robotics labs

universities

corporate boardrooms

government agencies

creative studios

The future belongs not to those who run from technology,
but to those who bring God's light into its deepest circuits.

8. Tech in God's Hands—And Ours

The future is not simply technological; it is spiritual.

AI will shape tomorrow,
but God shapes eternity.

The question is not whether AI has power—
but whether humanity will use that power with integrity.

The question is not whether tech can transform the world—
but whether God's people will guide that transformation.

When innovation serves love,
when algorithms reflect justice,
when progress honors dignity,
when wisdom directs creativity—

tech becomes part of God's instrument for redemption.

Scripture Reflections
Micah 6:8

"Do justice, love mercy, walk humbly with your God."

The ultimate guide for ethical AI.

James 1:5

"If any of you lacks wisdom, let him ask God…"

Wisdom must govern technology.

Proverbs 16:3

"Commit to the Lord whatever you do, and He will establish your plans."

Innovation anchored in God becomes secure.

Closing: A Future Held in Faith, Powered Through Purpose

Technology will continue evolving.
AI will grow smarter.
Systems will grow more powerful.
The world will change faster than ever.

But God remains unchanging.
And as long as humanity keeps its heart aligned with Him, the future need not be feared.

Tech in God's hands becomes:

a tool for justice

a vessel for grace

a channel for healing

a platform for truth

a bridge for unity

a reflection of His creativity

**The future guided by faith is bright—
not because AI is flawless,
but because God is faithful.**

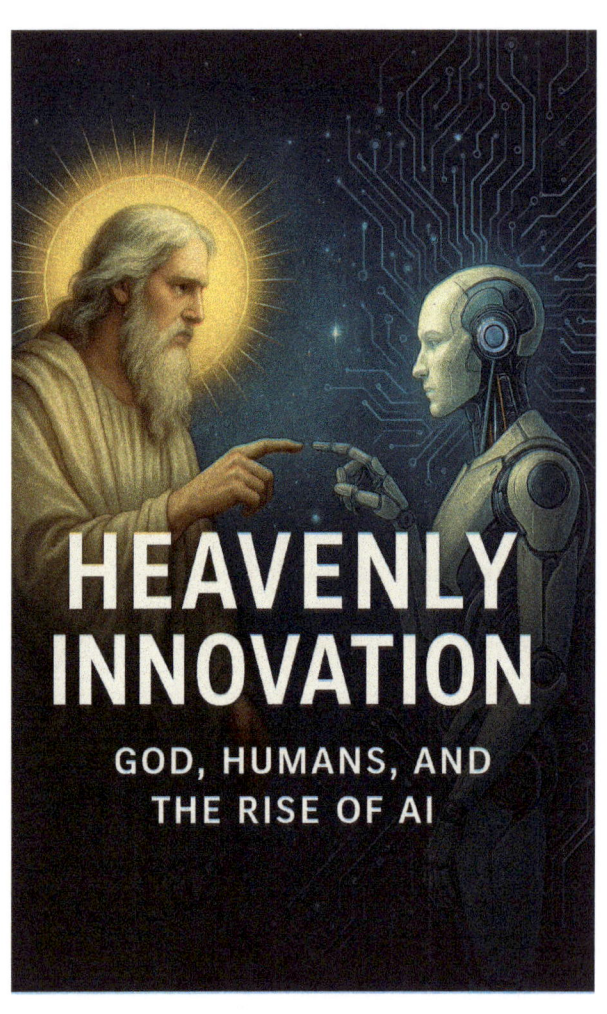

17. Heavenly Innovation: God, Humans, and the Rise of AI

Chapter 17

Heavenly Innovation: God, Humans, and the Rise of AI

Opening: A New Kind of Creation Story

In the beginning, God created the heavens and the earth.
In our time, humanity has created something far smaller but still astonishing:

Artificial Intelligence — a new kind of innovation born from minds that God Himself designed.

Humanity has always invented, imagined, and built. But AI represents a shift so significant that it feels almost biblical — a new chapter in the long story of how humans participate in God's creative work.

This chapter explores how God, humanity, and intelligent technology intersect, and why the rise of AI may not be a threat to faith but a continuation of the divine narrative.

1. Innovation Begins With God

Before humanity ever invented tools, systems,

or algorithms, God invented:

language

mathematics

logic

creativity

consciousness

intelligence

imagination

Every innovation humanity produces is possible only because God crafted human minds with the ability to think, reason, and design.

James 1:17

"Every good and perfect gift is from above…"

Innovation is one of those gifts.

Human ingenuity reflects divine ingenuity — not as equals, but as mirrors of God's creative image.

AI, therefore, is not outside of God's story.
It is part of it.

2. Humanity as Co-Creators With the Creator

God didn't simply place humans in creation as observers — He placed them there as builders.

Genesis 2:15

"The LORD God took the man and put him in the garden to work it and take care of it."

Work.
Cultivate.
Invent.
Shape.
Improve.

These were not expressions of rebellion — they were expressions of obedience.

AI emerges from the same mandate.
It is the modern extension of humanity's ancient mission:
to cultivate creation with wisdom and creativity.

We are not rivals to God.

We are stewards working under Him.

3. The Rise of AI: Not a Mistake, But a Moment

Some fear AI as if it slipped into the world without divine permission.

But if God is sovereign, then nothing — including AI — exists outside His allowance.

AI arises because:

God gave humans intelligence

humans sought to understand creation

curiosity, creativity, and exploration are built into us

technology progresses as knowledge grows

AI is not an accident.
It is a moment — a point in history where humanity's creative potential reaches a new height.
The rise of AI forces us to ask deeper questions about morality, responsibility, and purpose — questions that ultimately draw us back to God.

4. AI Is Powerful — But Not All-Powerful

Modern culture sometimes speaks about AI with awe, even fear.
But AI lacks everything that defines divinity:

AI is not eternal

AI is not sovereign

AI is not conscious

AI cannot create life

AI cannot love

AI cannot forgive

AI cannot know God

AI is powerful, but it is not holy.
Impressive, but not alive.
Intelligent, but not spiritual.

Technology can imitate the works of God, but it cannot imitate the heart of God.

5. The Divine Blueprint: God Above, Humans Between, Technology Below

In the proper order of creation:

God creates humanity
(with soul, spirit, purpose, and intelligence)

Humanity creates technology
(with creativity and reason)

Technology serves humanity
(as a tool, not a master)

This hierarchy is essential.

When reversed — when technology becomes our master, or when humans try to become gods — confusion and chaos follow.

Heavenly innovation requires keeping the divine blueprint intact.

6. AI as a Tool for God's Purposes

AI can participate, indirectly, in God's purposes when guided by faithful hearts.
AI can support God's work through:
Healing

diagnosing diseases

predicting medical risks

designing personalized treatments

Wisdom

revealing patterns in creation

assisting researchers and theologians

analyzing complex global systems

Justice

detecting fraud and corruption

helping prevent human trafficking

exposing systemic inequality

Compassion

supporting mental health care

aiding the disabled

assisting the elderly

Connection

translating Scripture

bridging language barriers

uniting communities

AI is not divine.
But it can amplify divine purposes in human hands.

7. The Spiritual Role of Humans in an AI World

The more AI advances, the more humanity must embrace:

moral leadership

spiritual grounding

compassionate decision-making

ethical responsibility
humility

AI can compute faster than we can —
but it cannot choose love.
It cannot choose righteousness.
It cannot choose God.

Humanity must remain the moral compass in

the age of algorithms.

God calls us not to fear the future, but to guide it.

8. Heavenly Innovation: When Technology Reflects God's Values

Technology becomes heavenly not when it is perfect, but when it is aligned with heaven's principles:

truth

justice

mercy

dignity

love
wisdom

stewardship

When innovation serves these principles, it brings heaven a little closer to earth.

Heavenly innovation happens whenever humans use God-given intelligence to build tools that uplift His creation.

Scripture Reflections
Psalm 8:5–6

"You made them rulers over the works of your hands."
AI is part of what we rule — not what rules us.

Proverbs 3:5–6

"In all your ways acknowledge Him…"
Innovation must bow before God, not replace Him.

Matthew 5:16

"Let your light shine before others…"
Let your creativity, your technology, your progress shine in ways that glorify God.
Closing: The Rise of AI and the Rise of Purpose

AI will not diminish God.
AI will not replace humanity.
AI will not rewrite creation.

Instead:

AI reveals humanity's potential,

and humanity reveals God's glory.

The question is not whether AI will change the world — it will.
The question is whether God's people will shape that change.

If we allow faith to guide innovation,
and allow God to guide both,
then the rise of AI becomes not a threat —
but a testimony.

A testimony that God's creativity is still unfolding through His people.

A testimony that heaven's influence can reach even into circuits and code.

A testimony that innovation, at its best, points back to the One who imagined everything first.

18. The Divine Partnership: How God Uses Technology for Good

Chapter 18

The Divine Partnership: How God Uses Technology for Good

Opening: When Human Innovation Meets Heavenly Purpose

Throughout history, God has chosen to work through people—and through the tools they create. The staff in Moses' hand, the sling in David's grip, the pen in Paul's fingers, the boat Jesus taught from—each was a simple tool transformed into an instrument of divine purpose.

Today, the tools look different.

Circuits. Algorithms. Sensors. Networks. And Artificial Intelligence.

But the truth remains unchanged:

God often works through human innovation to accomplish heavenly purposes.

This chapter explores how technology becomes part of God's plan for good—when it is placed, like everything else, in His hands.

1. A God Who Partners With Human Creativity

God could act alone.
Yet Scripture repeatedly shows Him choosing partnership.

God + Moses → liberation
God + Noah → preservation
God + David → victory
God + the Apostles → transformation of the world

The pattern is unmistakable:

God invites humanity not just to witness His work,
but to participate in it.

Technology simply gives humans new ways to join His mission.

Just as ancient tools amplified God's work in ancient times, modern tools can amplify God's work today.

2. The Misconception: "Technology Is Secular"

Many believe technology belongs to the

secular world and faith belongs to the spiritual world. But God does not divide the world into sacred and secular compartments.

Everything in creation—and everything created from creation—falls under His rule.

Psalm 24:1

"The earth is the Lord's, and everything in it."

If everything belongs to God, then innovation does too.

AI, robotics, medicine, data science, communication platforms…
All of it exists within God's realm.

There is no technology so advanced that it stands outside His sovereignty.

3. God Uses Technology to Heal

Jesus healed with a touch.
Today, healing often flows through machines, scans, medicine, and algorithms.

AI can:

- detect cancer earlier
- predict heart disease
- design personalized treatments
- monitor patients remotely
- support mental health care

When technology relieves suffering and restores life, it echoes the ministry of Jesus—who healed everywhere He went.

God has always been a healer. Technology becomes another tool in His hands.

4. God Uses Technology to Protect

From early-warning systems for natural disasters to AI that detects online predators, technology can defend the vulnerable.

AI can:

- prevent human trafficking
- detect fraud and corruption

- monitor abusive behavior

- alert authorities before danger escalates

- strengthen infrastructure safety

This reflects God's character as:

- protector of the weak

- defender of the oppressed

- guardian of justice

Technology becomes righteous when it shields those who cannot shield themselves.

5. God Uses Technology to Teach and Spread Truth

The printing press accelerated the spread of Scripture across continents.

Today's digital tools multiply that power a thousandfold.

AI can:

- translate the Bible into languages without

written systems

provide biblical resources to remote regions

create study tools for discipleship

strengthen churches with administrative support

offer encouragement and prayer reminders

Truth spreads faster than ever—not despite technology, but because of it.

God uses the tools of every age to communicate His message.

6. God Uses Technology to Unite People

At Babel, humanity misused technology to glorify themselves, and God scattered them. But at Pentecost, God reversed fragmentation by giving the disciples a divine "translation" tool—the ability to speak every language.

Today, technology echoes that miracle.

AI translation, global video calls, and digital community tools break barriers and heal divisions.

Used responsibly, technology can reflect God's desire for unity.

7. Technology as a Catalyst for Compassion

AI is not just about efficiency; it can be about empathy—when guided by purpose.

Technology can:

help caregivers assist the elderly

provide companionship to the isolated

support people with disabilities

identify communities in need

mobilize rapid responses to crises

Compassion—one of God's most defining attributes—can be amplified through innovation.

8. The Divine Partnership Requires Human Responsibility

God works through technology,
but He holds humanity accountable for how it is used.

The questions God asks are not:

"How advanced is the tech?"

"How powerful is the AI?"

Instead, God asks:

"Does it serve love?"

"Does it promote justice?"

"Does it protect the vulnerable?"

"Does it reflect truth?"

"Does it honor human dignity?"

Technology becomes dangerous when it becomes detached from morality.
But in the hands of the faithful, it becomes holy.

9. God Shapes the Future—Not Technology Alone

The rise of AI feels monumental, but God—not algorithms—shapes destiny.

AI may predict trends, but God directs history.
AI may change workflows, but God changes hearts.
AI may accelerate progress, but God defines purpose.

The future belongs to God.
Innovation simply becomes another vessel for His unfolding plan.

Scripture Reflections
Proverbs 16:3

"Commit to the Lord whatever you do, and He will establish your plans."
Technology guided by God becomes secure and fruitful.

Micah 6:8

"Do justice, love mercy, walk humbly."
The divine criteria for technology's moral purpose.

Ephesians 2:10

"We are His workmanship, created… to do good works."
Technology can help fulfill those good works.

Closing: When Technology Becomes an Instrument of Grace

Technology is not divine.
But it can be divinely used.

It is not holy.
But it can be made holy through purpose.

It is not alive.
But it can support life, protect life, and enhance life.

The Divine Partnership is this:
God provides wisdom.
Humanity provides creativity.
Technology becomes the bridge between the two.

In the hands of those guided by faith,
innovation becomes more than progress—
it becomes ministry.

More than invention—
it becomes compassion.

**More than advancement—
it becomes a testimony that God still works
through His people,
and through the tools they build.**

Chapter 19: Faith in the Future: God's Vision for AI and Humanity

Chapter 19

Faith in the Future: God's Vision for AI and Humanity

Opening: Tomorrow Is Not Unknown to God

The future may feel uncertain to humanity, but it is never uncertain to God. As technology accelerates and Artificial Intelligence reshapes daily life, people ask:

What will happen to humanity?

What will technology become?

How does faith fit into a digital future?

Is God still in control?

The answer is clear and eternal:

God has always held the future.
And He still does.

AI may be new to us, but not to Him.
Technological change may be shocking to us, but not to Him.
God's vision for humanity has never shifted.

This chapter explores what the future looks like when guided by God's wisdom—and how AI becomes part of a future where faith, not fear, leads the way.

1. God Already Stands in the Future

We often talk about the future as a distant, unexplored place.
But for God, the future is not ahead of Him—it is beneath Him.

Isaiah 46:10

"I make known the end from the beginning…"

Before the first circuit was designed,
before the first algorithm ran,
before the first AI system learned,

God already knew every outcome.

This means:

AI will never surprise God

human innovation will never outrun His sovereignty

nothing we build can step outside His authority

Faith in the future begins with faith in God's timelessness.

2. Humanity and AI Are Not Opponents

Some fear that AI will overpower humanity. But Scripture teaches that humans hold a unique, God-given identity that no machine can copy.

Humans alone:

are made in God's image

have souls

possess eternal purpose

understand morality

form relationships

can choose love

can choose God

AI cannot—ever—replace or diminish humanity's value.

Where machines simulate, humans experience. Where machines calculate, humans connect. Where machines imitate intelligence, humans embody spirit.

God's vision is not for AI to replace humanity, but to assist humanity.

3. Technology Will Increase—But So Will Purpose

Innovation has always risen throughout history:

tools

writing

agriculture

medicine

industry

electricity

computers

the internet

AI

Each technological wave expanded humanity's ability to shape God's world.

The rise of AI is simply the next chapter.

But the purpose remains the same:

**To serve.

**To heal.
To build.
To steward.
To uplift.
To honor God's creation.****

God's vision for the future involves humans using technology to amplify His goodness on earth.

4. The Future God Desires: Justice, Wisdom, and Compassion

The future is not defined by faster machines—

it is defined by deeper values.

Justice

AI used to fight corruption, expose injustice, and protect the vulnerable.

Wisdom

AI used responsibly by humans who pray, discern, and seek God's guidance.

Compassion

AI supporting the lonely, sick, disabled, and marginalized.

Unity

AI breaking language barriers and fostering global understanding.

Truth

AI elevating honesty, integrity, and clarity over deceit.

When technology reflects God's heart, the future becomes brighter, not darker.

5. God's Vision Is for Partnership, Not Fear

Fear is never God's starting point.

2 Timothy 1:7

"For God has not given us a spirit of fear…"

A fear-based future imagines:

AI as a threat

technology as uncontrollable

humanity as powerless

God as distant

But a faith-based future recognizes:

AI as a tool

technology as God-allowed

humanity as responsible

God as fully in control

Faith removes fear and replaces it with clarity:

We are not spectators to the future.
We are partners in shaping it.

6. The Role of Believers in a Technological Age

God calls His people to lead—not withdraw.

Believers must:

guide ethical conversations

build compassionate technologies

champion human dignity

protect the vulnerable

confront injustice

advocate for truth

model humility

design systems that reflect God's values

Christians have shaped culture for thousands of years—through art, science, law, medicine, and education.

The future of AI should be no different.

Faith-filled people must step into the digital arena and lead with integrity.

7. What the Future Looks Like Under God's Guidance

When faith guides AI, the future includes:

- **Healing without borders**

AI-assisted medicine reaching remote places.

- **Education for every child**

AI tutoring and accessible learning tools.

- **Justice that transcends bias**

AI detecting inequality and abuse.

- **Compassion scaled globally**

Technology supporting care, inclusion, and well-being.

- **Truth that shines**

AI helping filter misinformation and amplify what is right.

- Human dignity protected

AI designed with fairness, transparency, and respect.

- Innovation anchored in wisdom

Tech development shaped by prayer, ethics, and humility.

In God's vision, technology becomes a multiplier of His goodness.

8. God Is Not Just in the Future—He Is in the Process

God's vision unfolds not only in the outcome but also in the creation:

in the designer writing ethical code

in the engineer solving a problem

in the doctor using AI to save a life

in the missionary using tools to spread hope

in the family using AI for learning and connection

God's presence is not limited to church walls. He works in labs, research centers, classrooms, and offices.

The future is holy not because of technology, but because of the God who guides it.

Scripture Reflections
Jeremiah 29:11

"For I know the plans I have for you… plans to give you hope and a future."

God's plans include every era—digital ones too.

Proverbs 3:5–6

"In all your ways acknowledge Him, and He will make straight your paths."

A roadmap for ethical innovation.

Psalm 33:11

"The plans of the LORD stand firm forever."

Even as technology changes daily, God's purposes remain eternal.

Closing: A Future Worth Believing In

AI will shape the future—but God shapes eternity.
Technology may transform life—but God transforms hearts.
The world may change rapidly—but God never changes.

The future God envisions is one where:

faith leads progress

humanity retains dignity

innovation serves goodness

wisdom guides decisions

justice protects the vulnerable

compassion inspires tools

truth prevails

God remains at the center

**Faith in the future is not wishful thinking—
it is confidence in the God who authored it.**

**With God guiding humanity,
and humanity guiding technology,
the future is not something to fear—
but something to build.**

Chapter 20:
Blessed Intelligence: AI as a Tool for God's Work

**Chapter 20

Blessed Intelligence: AI as a Tool for God's Work**

Opening: When Innovation Becomes an Instrument of Heaven

Every generation receives tools suited for its mission. In ancient days, God used staffs, slings, arks, temples, scrolls, and sails to carry out His purposes.
Today, the tools look different: microchips, datasets, algorithms, neural networks, and Artificial Intelligence systems.

But the principle remains:

When placed in God's hands, tools become instruments of blessing.
Even intelligent technology.

AI is not simply a technical achievement—it is a platform through which God can extend healing, justice, compassion, and truth into a world desperately in need of all four.

This chapter explores how AI can become blessed intelligence—not divine, not sacred in itself, but divinely used when guided by God's people.

1. God Works Through Human Creation

Scripture shows a consistent pattern:
God accomplishes His work through the creativity He gave humanity.

God told Noah how to build the ark.

God inspired Bezalel with artistic skill for the Tabernacle.

God guided the engineers of Solomon's Temple.

God used letters and ink to spread the Gospel.

At every step, human ingenuity served divine purpose.

AI is simply the newest canvas on which God can paint His intentions through willing hands.

Human innovation is not separate from God's work—
it is one of the ways He partners with

humanity.

2. Intelligence Is Blessed When It Serves God's Heart

Intelligence—human or artificial—is never holy by nature.
It becomes holy when it:

uplifts the suffering

pursues justice

reveals truth

protects the vulnerable

strengthens communities

expands knowledge

reflects God's compassion

Blessed intelligence is intelligence aligned with God's values.

The question is not whether AI is good or evil; the question is whether the people guiding it align it with God's purposes.

3. AI as a Tool for Healing

Jesus healed with compassion and power. Today, medical AI carries that same spirit forward by:

diagnosing illnesses earlier than ever

predicting diseases before symptoms appear

supporting doctors in complex surgeries

monitoring patients remotely

analyzing genetic disorders

AI is not performing miracles,
but it is helping extend the healing ministry of Christ through the hands of doctors and researchers.

Healing is God's work.
AI can help accomplish it.

4. AI as a Tool for Justice

God's heart beats for justice.

Psalm 82:3

"Defend the weak and the fatherless; uphold the cause of the poor and oppressed."

AI can assist this divine mandate by:

detecting trafficking networks

identifying financial fraud

analyzing criminal patterns

exposing corruption

promoting fair, unbiased decision systems

alerting authorities to dangerous activity

When used with integrity, AI becomes a shield for the vulnerable.

Justice is God's work.
AI can help carry it out.

5. AI as a Tool for Compassion

Compassion was the hallmark of Jesus' ministry.

Today, AI is helping extend compassion by:

offering support to people dealing with loneliness

assisting caregivers for the elderly

helping people with disabilities communicate

providing mental health tools

identifying communities in crisis

Technology can never replace human love, but it can support and amplify it.

Compassion is God's work.
AI can help nurture it.

6. AI as a Tool for Truth

In a world full of misinformation, AI can help:

detect false news

preserve historical accuracy

promote clarity

filter harmful content

build trustworthy systems of knowledge

support biblical education and translation

Truth is a core value of God's character.

John 14:6

"I am the way, the truth, and the life."

AI cannot create truth,
but it can help safeguard it.

7. AI as a Tool to Expand God's Kingdom

The early church used parchment and roads to spread the Gospel.
The Reformation used the printing press.
Modern churches use livestreams and digital study tools.

AI takes this even further:

translating Scripture into languages with no written resources

supporting missionaries with cultural training

creating Bible study tools for every age

reaching isolated communities

accelerating theological research

providing encouragement and prayer through digital platforms

When used wisely, AI becomes a megaphone for God's message.

Evangelism is God's work.
AI can help amplify it.

8. AI Becomes Dangerous When Detached From God

Blessing requires alignment.

If AI is used for selfishness, exploitation, deception, or domination, it no longer serves God's purpose.

Blessed intelligence becomes broken intelligence when:

pride drives decisions

ethics are ignored

truth is distorted

human dignity is compromised

technology is used to replace God or humanity

AI must always remain under human control, and humanity must remain under God's authority.

Without that hierarchy, technology loses its blessing.

9. The Divine Partnership Requires Human Stewardship

God may use technology for good,
but He expects humans to steward it responsibly.

AI must be guided by:

prayer

ethical principles

compassion

humility

justice

Scripture

accountability

Blessed AI requires blessed leadership.

When human hearts align with God, human tools align with His will.

10. Blessed Intelligence: The Future God Invites Us Into

God's plan for AI is not fear-based but faith-filled.

In God's hands, AI can help:

heal diseases

feed families

educate children

protect communities

translate Scriptures

prevent disasters

restore hope

strengthen churches

uplift nations

AI cannot replace God,
but God can use AI.

That is blessed intelligence.

Scripture Reflections
James 1:5

"If any of you lacks wisdom, let him ask God…"
AI requires wisdom beyond algorithms.

Colossians 3:23

"Whatever you do, do it for the Lord."
Even innovation can be an act of worship.

Ephesians 2:10

"Created… to do good works."
Technology can help accomplish those works.

Closing: Tools in Our Hands, Power in His

AI is a tool.
God is the source.
We are the stewards.

When AI is guided by faith,
it becomes more than a technological achievement—
it becomes an extension of God's goodness in the world.

Blessed intelligence is not about the machine.
It is about the mission.

Not about what AI knows,
but what God does through it.

Not about artificial power,
but about divine purpose.

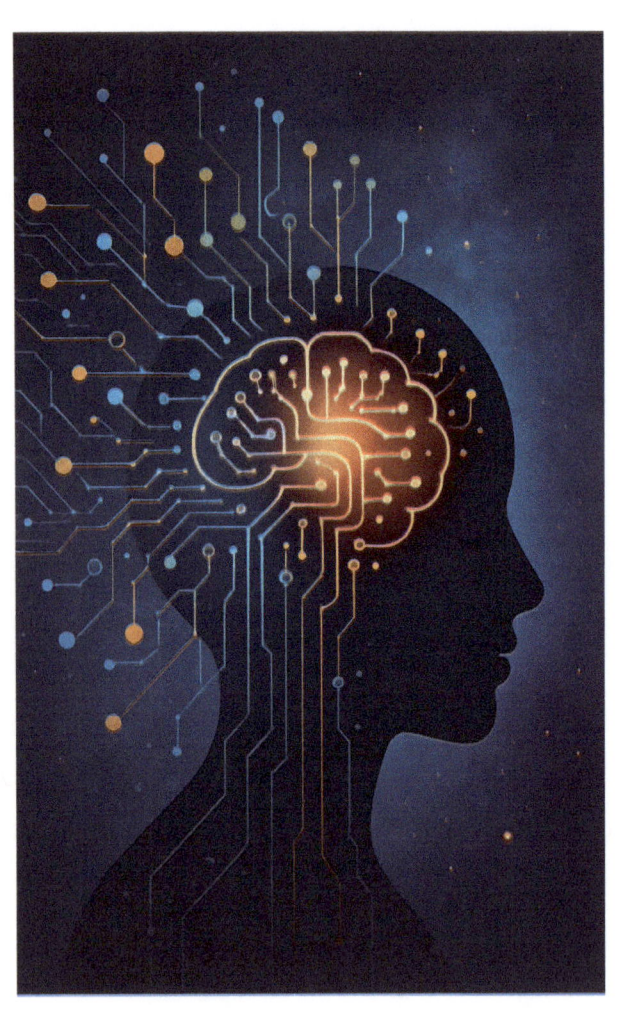

About The Photographs:

The images featured throughout AI Predictions for 2026 were created in collaboration with advanced artificial intelligence illustration tools, guided by the creative direction of author Robert Armstrong. Each visual was intentionally crafted to reflect the spirit of innovation, transformation, and human-AI partnership explored in the book's chapters.

Rather than merely decorating the pages, these images serve as visual gateways into the future—capturing imagined technologies, emotional landscapes, and the evolving relationship between humanity and intelligent machines. From depictions of mainstream AI breakthroughs to energetic portrayals of personal AI companions, healthcare revolutions, and creative collaboration, every illustration supports the book's mission: to make complex ideas vivid, accessible, and inspiring.

By blending human creativity with AI-generated artistry, the imagery mirrors the very theme of the book—a future where humans and intelligent systems co-create new possibilities. These visuals are a testament to what collaborative intelligence can produce when imagination, technology, and storytelling come together.

Photographs Copyright Statement:

The illustrations in this book were created by Robert Armstrong in collaboration with advanced artificial intelligence image-generation tools. Each image is considered an original creative work and is fully protected under United States and international copyright laws.

No part of the visual content—whether images, graphics, or design elements—may be reproduced, stored in a retrieval system, transmitted, or distributed in any form or by any means (electronic, mechanical, photocopying, recording, or otherwise) without prior written permission from the copyright holder.

Unauthorized use, duplication, or adaptation of these images is strictly prohibited.

For permissions or licensing inquiries, please contact: Robert Armstrong / US Value Core LLC LibraryUserGroup.com

About The Author:

Robert Armstrong is a visionary storyteller, entrepreneur, and creative architect whose work spans multiple genres—from heartwarming children's tales and imaginative mysteries to insightful explorations of technology, resilience, and human potential. His unique ability to blend emotional depth with forward-thinking ideas has earned him recognition as a writer who inspires, uplifts, and ignites curiosity in readers of all ages.

Armstrong's literary voice is distinguished by its compassion and clarity. Whether he is guiding a young reader through a playful adventure, crafting an empowering journal, unveiling a clever mystery featuring characters like Maddy and Amanda, or unpacking the profound implications of artificial intelligence, his writing reflects a deep understanding of the human spirit. His characters—children, families, dreamers, innovators, and everyday heroes—mirror the hopes, challenges, and transformations that shape our lives.

Beyond fiction, Armstrong is also known for his compelling nonfiction works, including AI Predictions for 2026, where he explores the evolving partnership between humanity and intelligent machines. His thoughtful approach to technological advancement emphasizes creativity, ethics, and the promise of a better future built through collaboration.

Armstrong's expansive creative universe includes educational workbooks, uplifting journals, story collections, character-driven mysteries, and innovative digital experiences powered through his brands Library User Group and US Value Core LLC. This ecosystem reflects his belief that stories—and the tools we use to tell them—can inspire learning, connect communities, and spark imagination across generations.

With each new book, Robert Armstrong invites readers on a journey of discovery, healing, growth, and innovation. His work stands as a testament to the enduring power of storytelling—and the extraordinary possibilities that emerge when creativity and technology come together.

CREATED IN HIS IMAGE — AI AND DIVINE BLUEPRINT	**FAITH IN AN AGE OF INTELLIGENT MACHINES** —	UNDERSTANDING AI THROUGH 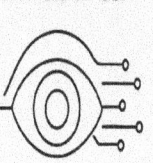 LEN?S
THE GOD ALGORITHM — FAITH IN AN AGE INTELLIGENT LENS 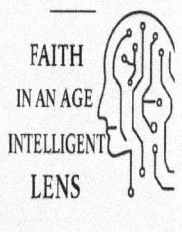	**IN GOD'S DESIGN** — UNDERSTANDING AI THROUGH A SPIRITUAL LENS	**SOUL OF THE MACHINE** — EXPLORING GOD'S VIEW OF AI

CREATED IN HIS IMAGE

AI AND DIVINE BLUEFRINT

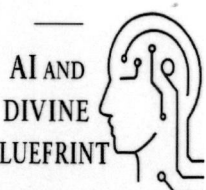

FAITH IN AN AGE OF INTELLIGENT MACHINES

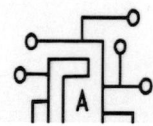

UNDERSTANDING AI THROUGH

LEN≷S

THE GOD ALGORITHM

FAITH IN AN AGE INTELLIGENT LENS

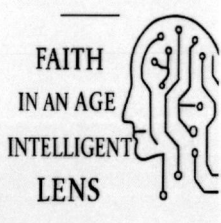

IN GOD'S DESIGN

UNDERSTANDING AI THROUGH A SPIRITUAL LENS

SOUL OF THE MACHINE

EXPLORING GOD'S VIEW OF AI

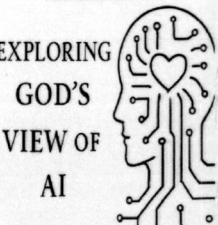

ISBN 978-1-63553-027-8
90000

9 781635 530278